BRENNAN AND DEMOCRACY

BRENNAN AND DEMOCRACY

Frank I. Michelman

PRINCETON UNIVERSITY PRESS   PRINCETON, NEW JERSEY

Copyright © 1999 by Princeton University Press
Published by Princeton University Press, 41 William Street,
Princeton, New Jersey 08540
In the United Kingdom: Princeton University Press,
Chichester, West Sussex
All Rights Reserved.

Library of Congress Cataloging-in-Publication Data
Michelman, Frank I., 1936–
Brennan and democracy / Frank I. Michelman
p.   cm.
Includes index.
ISBN 0-691-00715-2 (cl : alk. paper)
1. Brennan, William J. (William Joseph), 1906—
2. Constitutional law—United States. I. Title.
KF8745.B68M53   1999
342.73—dc21   98-43565   CIP

This book has been composed in Janson

The paper used in this publication meets the minimum requirements
of ANSI/NISO Z39.48-1992 (R1997) (*Permanence of Paper*)

http://pup.princeton.edu

1   3   5   7   9   10   8   6   4   2
Printed in the United States of America

For the Justice — the Boss — Bill — and
All Who Loved Him

Contents

Preface and Acknowledgments

CHAPTER 1 of this book is adapted from my essay, "Brennan and Democracy," prepared for the first Brennan Center Symposium on Constitutional Law, held twice in 1996–97 at the University of California, Berkeley, School of Law, and the New York University School of Law.[1] Chapter 2 is adapted from my 1990 McCorkle Lecture, "Super Liberal," delivered at the University of Virginia School of Law.[2] Both chapters consider, in quite different ways, the significance for American constitutional thought and practice of the judicial career of Justice William J. Brennan, Jr. In chapter 1, Brennan figures thematically, as an exemplar of a contentious conception of the role of a constitutional judge in a democracy and a name for one side of a divided mind. In chapter 2, he becomes the holder of a specific set of substantive political ideas that motivate his judgeship. Having thus treated of Brennan the model for thought and Brennan the actor in history, I have also included, as an Epilogue, a few pages closely drawn from my contribution to the Harvard Law Review's recent collection of memorials for Justice Brennan,[3] where I have something to say about William Brennan the person.

I served as one of Brennan's law clerks in 1961–62 and I initially set out to collect these pieces into a small book as my act of tribute to a man I loved and enormously esteemed. But I quickly formed the desire to make the memorial a living one, by putting the Brennan record to work in aid of two quite different projects: acquainting a general readership with some aspects of an academic specialty called "constitutional theory," and saying something on behalf of liberalism as a contender in the current political contro-

---

[1] See Frank I. Michelman, "Brennan and Democracy," *California Law Review* 86 (1998): 399–427.

[2] See Frank I. Michelman, "Super Liberal," *Virginia Law Review* 77 (1991): 1261–1332.

[3] See "In Memoriam—William J. Brennan, Jr., *Harvard Law Review* 111 (1997): 1–50. My contribution appears at pp. 37–40.

versies of this country. I hope that chapter 1 might prompt a non-specialist audience to reflect on how tough and delicate an act it is that Americans undertake by attempting to live as a self-governing people, yet under a rule of law—a kind of reflection that in my own case has been prompted in no small measure, as I explain, by Brennan's example. I hope that chapter 2 might prompt a nonspecialist audience to a renewed appreciation of the attractions and strengths of democratic liberal political ideals.

These objectives have led to substantial rewriting of the two main chapters, initially prepared as works of scholarship for a mainly specialist audience. Converting them for a more general readership has meant purging the material of citations and side discussions that serve important purposes in scholarly exchange—to take a point to a further degree of refinement or precision, to open for discussion a new question that one is not prepared to try to answer, to locate one's work in relation to that of other scholars—but that could only be distractions and annoyances for nonspecialists. It has also meant adding explanations of insider stuff: legal and academic terms, concepts, allusions, doctrines, and debates. Once the process of revision was started, I did not resist temptations to edit, to reorganize, and even to substitute lengthy passages of freshly written material.

There nevertheless remains an important sense in which the material is dated, especially that in chapter 2, which I wrote in 1990–91. That chapter is a record and a rendition of Justice Brennan's political thought as mainly expressed by him in the course of a judicial career that came to an end in 1990. I have made no attempt to carry down to date any of the judicial, civic, or academic controversies that are presented in the chapter.

A word of explanation about the ordering of the two main chapters will aid the reader at the outset. Despite their quite different focal questions—What is the relationship between political democracy and limited rulership by judges? What conception of a good, democratic society inspired William Brennan's exercise of limited judicial rulership?—they help explain each other. No one should feel bound to read them in the order in which I finally, after much wavering, decided to place them in this volume. If you prefer to start with something relatively concrete before moving to something relatively abstract, begin with chapter 2.

Brennan is not the only major player in these pages. I am here, too, plying my trade as constitutional theorist, and even trying to be (not my day job) a bit of a political propagandist. The mixture could put at some risk the part of this—the bulk of it—that is supposed to describe Brennan and not me. "How can I tell," you might reasonably ask yourself, "when this guy is just writing down lines he likes and popping them into Brennan's head?" The answer is, I will tell you. Whenever and to the extent that I want to say that Brennan thought something or meant something, that is exactly what I *will* say. If I don't expressly say it, then I'm not claiming it, or even suggesting or slyly insinuating it.

Overall, I have not looked for evidence to support my accounts of Brennan's most general political and jurisprudential stances and outlooks apart from things he said about other matters, more concrete, in and by his judicial opinions and decisions. Distilling broader motivating ideas from another's more concretely directed words and acts is—as Justice Brennan knew—a sort of work from which one cannot possibly seal out one's own ideas about the same topics. Nevertheless, there is a difference between a reading of another's words and acts and a substitution for them of whatever *you* think is right, and I have meant to respect that difference.

I cannot possibly name everyone who has helped me clarify and advance my thoughts about the matters treated here. I am particularly grateful to Ronald Dworkin, Don Herzog, Robert Post, and Kathleen Sullivan, the four appointed commentators for the Brennan Symposium Lecture that became chapter 1. Their attentive and incisive comments helped me to improve the work considerably.[4] I have learned a great deal more from extended e-mail correspondence about these matters with Robert

---

[4] The published comments of Professors Dworkin, Herzog, Post, and Sullivan, along with my rejoinders, can be found in the *California Law Review* immediately following my Lecture.

Post. Professors James Fleming, Larry Kramer, and Kenneth Winston also gave valuable comments on prior versions of chapter 1. C. Edwin Baker, William W. Fisher III, Andrew Kaufman, and Martha Minow all gave helpful advice on chapter 2 when I was preparing that material for the first time in 1990–91.

Sharon McGowan of the Harvard Law School class of 2000 and E. Joshua Rosenkranz of the Brennan Center for Justice read the entire manuscript. Both offered much good advice about clarification and expansion of a number of points. Josh Rosenkranz has been a support and inspiration throughout.

The Brennan Center Symposiums on Constitutional Law are sponsored by the Brennan Center for Justice at the New York University School of Law and funded by a gift from Professor Thomas Jorde of the University of California at Berkeley School of Law. I am indebted for the opportunity to Professor Jorde, the Center, and the two host schools.

Finally, I am grateful to the Harvard Law School and its dean, Robert C. Clark, for summer research support.

Portions of chapter 1 originally appeared in my "Brennan and Democracy" and "Rejoinders," 86 *California Law Review* 399, 469 (1998) and are reprinted by permission of the California Law Review, Inc. Portions of chapter 2 originally appeared in my "Super Liberal," 77 *Virginia Law Review* 1261 (1991) and are reprinted by permission of the Virginia Law Review Association.

BRENNAN AND DEMOCRACY

Brennan's Constitutional Democracy

CONSTITUTIONAL LAW, CONSTITUTIONAL THEORY

In American law schools today, cheek-by-jowl with the study and teaching of constitutional law, you find a sibling branch of academic exertion called "constitutional theory." What's the difference?

It all starts with judicial review, that noteworthy practice of American government by which unelected judges hear and decide cases of complaint—"it's unconstitutional"—against laws enacted by electorally accountable legislatures. Unmistakably, these are legal cases, in which judges explain and justify their decisions with the same sorts of arguments about the best interpretations of legal texts and precedents that lawyers use in urging the decisions they favor. How much these legal arguments *cause* the decisions of judges and how much they merely decorate them is unknown. What is clear is that many people think it practically worthwhile to acquire a professional, insider knowledge of the materials—the legal texts, precedents, and doctrines—to which lawyers and judges refer in these cases, along with knowledge of the conventional codes and understandings that guide and ease professional exchange about the materials, the history of professional debate about their origins and meanings, and the relevant dispositions toward them of currently sitting judges. Such knowledge can become subtle and deep. Acquiring, refining, and conveying it is the business of the academic field of constitutional law. But then what is left for "constitutional theory?"

Most people who study constitutional law with much seriousness do so with the purpose of getting good at doing it as lawyers do it, or teaching others to do so. Constitutional theorists study constitutional law for a different purpose. Their concern is to explain, and perhaps to justify, an apparently undemocratic practice of government "by judiciary"[1] in which popular political outcomes are subjected to the test of a judicially administered "higher" law. Having learned enough (they think) about the specifically American version of this practice and the texts, doctrines, methods, debates, institutions, and conventions that go to make it up, constitutional theorists look behind the practice for normative principles that can justify, or beliefs that can explain, our country's use of it as a part of its system of government. Having found out (they hope) the motivating principles and beliefs, constitutional theorists may then want to use them prescriptively, as a guide to future resolution of debated questions about either the meaning of the Constitution or the right method for finding out that meaning. More radically, the theorist may want to reveal the poverty of the principles or the lunacy of the beliefs as a reason for wholesale abandonment of the practice of subjecting the outcomes of popular government to any further legal test.

THE PARADOX OF CONSTITUTIONAL DEMOCRACY

American constitutional theory is eternally hounded, if not totally consumed, by a search for harmony between what are usually heard as two clashing commitments: one to the ideal of government constrained by law ("constitutionalism"), the other to the ideal of government by act of the people ("democracy"). The search is one with which no partisan of democracy can proceed today without reckoning with the judicial career of William Brennan.

---

[1] "Government by judiciary" appears in the titles of two books that I know of, but neither author appears to give a source. See Raoul Berger, *Government By Judiciary: The Transformation of the Fourteenth Amendment* (Cambridge, Mass.:

Do you see some slight to democracy—some "Counter-Majoritarian Difficulty," to recall Professor Alexander Bickel's famous phrase—in unelected judges ruling the country, in part, by passing on the legal validity of laws duly enacted by elected representatives?[2] If you do, then William Brennan before all other American judges must personify the Difficulty you see. He was our generation's model "activist" constitutional judge and, indeed, American history's activist judge without peer except for the early great Chief Justice, John Marshall. That makes it something of a curiosity to find, among crowds of hand-wringers over the country's submission to undemocratic government by judiciary, a good many of us who also greatly admire and loudly applaud Brennan's judicial career. It would seem we owe ourselves and others some explanation. Are we, after all, as serious as we claim to be about democracy? Being myself caught in this compromising position, I felt it was right, on an occasion of academic exchange in Justice Brennan's honor,[3] to return once more to the question that keeps the Constitutional Theory department in business: Brennan and democracy—how to have both?

This chapter ends with a surmise about what might have been Brennan's own answer to the question, drawn from his words and deeds. As we proceed, though, I shall be at least as intent on getting you to see how hard and deep and relentless the question really is. I shall speak repeatedly of a "paradox" of constitutional democracy. The paradox assumes various guises, but let us start with its simplest version, its normal form.

"Democracy" appears to mean something like this: Popular political self-government—the people of a country deciding for

Harvard University Press, 1977); Louis Boudin, *Government By Judiciary* (New York: W. Godwin, 1932), 12.

[2] Alexander M. Bickel, *The Least Dangerous Branch: The Supreme Court at the Bar of Politics* (Indianapolis: Bobbs-Merrill, 1962), 16–23.

[3] I originally prepared this chapter for the first annual Brennan Center Symposium on Constitutional Law. The Symposiums are sponsored by the Brennan Center for Justice at the New York University School of Law and are funded by a gift from Professor Thomas Jorde of the University of California at Berkeley School of Law.

themselves the contents (especially, one would think, the most fateful and fundamental contents) of the laws that organize and regulate their political association. "Constitutionalism" appears to mean something like this: The containment of popular political decision-making by a basic law, the Constitution—a "law of lawmaking," we shall sometimes call it—designed to control which further laws can be made, by whom, and by what procedures. It is, of course, an essential part of the notion of constitutionalism that the basic law must be untouchable by the majoritarian politics it is meant to contain. (If ordinary political majorities could fiddle with it, it wouldn't be doing its job of containment.)

If these two rough definitions fairly capture what we mean by "democracy" and "constitutionalism," then attempts to fold the two principles into one ideal conception of a political order do indeed appear to be headed for trouble. To see this, it will be helpful to define a category of "politically decidable" questions. A question is politically decidable, let us say, if it is the sort of question that *can* be settled by the act of some political ruler or the vote of some body such as Congress or the electorate. I mean "can" in a plain, practical sense. Thus, a very clear case of something that is politically decidable is a question about what the law of some country shall be. We have no trouble at all with the idea that a country's law really is whatever a vote of some body (Congress, the electorate) from time to time decides it shall be. By contrast, everyone would agree that the force of gravity is not politically decidable, and most would agree that neither is the beauty of a poem.

We can now say that, by the principle of democracy, the people of a country ought to decide for themselves all of the politically decidable matters about which they have good moral and material reason to care. That apparently must include the contents of a country's constitution, the laws that organize the institutions of government and set limits to governmental powers in that country. These obviously are politically decidable matters, about which a country's people obviously do have strong reason to care. And yet these are the very laws of lawmaking that must lie beyond the reach of majority ("political") decision if constitutionalism is truly in force.

The full implications of these remarks will emerge as we go along. For now, though, just consider the following illustrative questions, all of them politically decidable:

- Shall there or shall there not be in force in your country a law of lawmaking that all but prohibits government from "affirmative action" or any other sort of race-conscious legislation or administration, in any circumstances, for any reason?
- Shall there or shall there not be in force in your country a law of lawmaking that narrowly restricts the ability of the government to regulate the flow of money in political campaigns?
- Shall there or shall there not be in force in your country a law of lawmaking that narrowly restricts the ability of government to regulate what people do about having sex, becoming pregnant, remaining pregnant, or becoming a parent?

The choices posed by such questions are so obviously important to so many people, materially and morally, that it seems they must fall within democracy's reach if we take democracy seriously at all. They are also quite unmistakably—I wrote them so that they would be—choices about the laws of lawmaking, and the principle of constitutionalism requires that at least some choices about the laws of lawmaking be placed securely beyond the reach of democratic politics to decide.

In this chapter, I want to push your sense of the paradox of constitutional democracy beyond the terms of "difficulty." The problem has a depth and a poignancy that we may not feel comfortable confronting, and Bickel's diplomatic phraseology lets us too easily off the hook. To say that difficulty stands in the way of a melding of constitutionalism with democracy is to imply that we can all the same do it if we keep our wits about us. But I think we learn more if we start by doubting systematically whether constitutional democracy is possible, at least insofar as we take the point of it all to have something to do with individual freedom and self-government. Doing so should chasten our imagining of, and our hopes for, all the ideals in play here—constitutionalism, democracy, and self-government.

That does not mean we give up the ideals. It does mean we never let ourselves forget that any society's goals respecting democracy, self-government, and a rule of law or of reason must be ones of approximation, of holding in check the misfortune of how things are, of choosing among necessarily compromised offerings of necessarily damaged goods. That is just a matter of social fact and the laws of logic, or so I mean to contend, and American constitutional democracy is not immune to fact and logic; it is not the little engine that could; we are not *that* exceptional. Teaching ourselves to see our country's constitutional democratic practices as, at their best, sisyphean attempts to approximate unsatisfiable ideals of democracy and self-government under law—not just technically, but logically and conceptually unsatisfiable—may help us steer clear of foolish acts and proposals in the name of ideals that we nevertheless have reason to continue to hold. It may also sharpen both appreciation and criticism of those practices, and of justification-intended interpretations of them such as those to be considered in this chapter.

Recall my illustrative list of politically decidable questions about the laws of lawmaking that one would expect the citizens of a democratically self-governing country to decide for themselves. In fact, those are all questions that the United States Supreme Court currently decides for this country, in the course of interpreting the country's established code of laws of lawmaking, the Constitution of the United States. The Court reads the Constitution practically to forbid state lawmakers from making the election of any number of persons of color an objective when drawing up legislative districts, and in general to impose very strict limits on the use by government agencies of affirmative action set-asides and quotas.[4] It reads the Constitution to prohibit Congress from restricting political campaign expenditures for the purpose of "equalizing" the voices of rich and poor people in the selection of government officials or the setting of government policy.[5] It reads the Constitution to prohibit states from restricting people's use of contraceptives[6] and from imposing undue burdens on a woman's freedom to choose to abort a pregnancy.[7]

In all of this, we confront a spectacle of judges outspokenly holding themselves responsible, according to what they take to be the very notion of constitutional government, to pronounce with finality on the content and meaning of the country's laws of lawmaking. The Supreme Court's opinion in *Cooper v. Aaron*, issued in the name of the Court as a whole but mainly written by Justice Brennan, declares the Justices "supreme in the exposition of the law of the Constitution."[8] Similarly, but even more assertively, the decisive opinion in a recent abortion case claims for

---

[4] See Adarand Constructors, Inc. v. Pena, 115 S. Ct. 2097 (1995); Miller v. Johnson, 115 S. Ct. 2475 (1995).

[5] See Buckley v. Valeo, 424 U.S. 1 (1976).

[6] See Griswold v. Connecticut, 381 U.S. 479 (1965); Eisenstadt v. Baird, 405 U.S. 438 (1972).

[7] See Planned Parenthood of Southeastern Pennsylvania v. Casey, 506 U.S. 833 (1992).

[8] 358 U.S. 1, 18 (1958). See also William J. Brennan, Jr., "The Equality Principle: A Foundation of American Law," *University of California at Davis Law Review* 20 (1987): 673–78, at 674: "In our society, it has historically been the courts that have interpreted and made acceptable [the commitment to a set of values contained in a] Rule of Law." *Cooper v. Aaron* was a case growing out of the decision of Arkansas Governor Orval Faubus to use the Arkansas National Guard to prevent black students from entering Little Rock Central High School in 1957 in accordance with a court-ordered desegregation plan, an action to which President Eisenhower eventually responded by sending in the U.S. Army and federalizing the Arkansas Guard. In the *Cooper* case, the Supreme Court made a swift and unanimous response—"No Way"—to a request of Little Rock school authorities for a postponement of compliance with the desegregation order, in view of public turmoil that they said had been stirred up by Faubus's actions. For Brennan's authorship of the Supreme Court's opinion, see Richard S. Arnold, "In Memoriam—William J. Brennan, Jr.," *Harvard Law Review* 11 (1997): 5–9, at 6–7.

the Court the role of "speak[ing] before all others" for "the constitutional *ideals*" (it's not enough for them just to speak for the laws) of the country. At stake in the Court's performance of this role, three Justices wrote, is Americans' "belief in themselves as a people who aspire to live according to the rule of law."[9] The authors of those judicial manifestos don't seem awfully worried about the country's people deciding for themselves the contents or even the spirit of the fundamental laws. Must we then count them as foes of democracy?

Not necessarily, it is said: they may be democracy's heroes, depending on the spirit and content that they by their interpretations accord to the laws of lawmaking. There are in circulation two main variations on this theme. One construes democracy as a matter of people actually having certain specific kinds of legal rights, the other construes it as a matter of the procedures we use to decide what legal rights people are to have. Each variation, providentially, has a champion among the constitutional theorists who served as commentators when I presented this material in lecture form—Ronald Dworkin for democracy-as-rights, Robert Post for democracy-as-procedure. I want to accompany each of those scholars on his tour from one of the poles of our terrain (democracy-as-rights, democracy-as-procedure) to the point where the two meet up in paradox.

Initially, though, I need to point out how controversial and problematic is the quest on which both venturers are embarked. Both pose for themselves what I suppose we can call Rousseau's problem—to find a form of political association, a set of arrangements for lawmaking, in which each individual human being remains or becomes his or her own governor, providing from within his or her own will and judgment the direction and regulation of his or her own life. The problem has proved to be an extremely puzzling one, and when Post and Dworkin delve into the relations

---

[9] Planned Parenthood of Southeastern Pennsylvania v. Casey, 505 U.S. 833, 868 (1992) (O'Connor, Kennedy, and Souter, J. J.) (emphasis supplied). For an endorsement, see Ronald Dworkin, *Life's Dominion: An Argument about Abortion, Euthanasia, and Individual Freedom* (New York: Knopf, 1993), 120, 126.

between democracy and constitutionalism, it is with a view to explaining how constitutional democracy can redeem an ideal of personal self-government in politics that has haunted, daunted, and taunted liberal thought for hundreds of years.

DEMOCRACY, INDIVIDUALS, AND SELF-GOVERNMENT

Self-Government and Individuals

What is the point of democracy? Why should you care about the establishment in your country of democratic political arrangements? No doubt, we care about this partly for reasons of accountability. We want the people's governors, whoever they are, to govern the people in accordance with the interests of the people. We think that if those who govern the people hold office on sufferance of popular majorities, and if the electoral and representational schemes for toting those majorities are geared to a fair reflection of interests in the population, then government probably will attend decently well to the interests of the governed. Thus, we will have government for the people.

But if Lincoln was right, Americans care about democracy for a further reason as well. We want government to be *by* the people as well as *for* them. A self-respecting people, we think, exercise their own charge over the politically decidable conditions of their lives. They thus realize, with respect to those conditions, that aspect of human dignity and freedom that philosophers sometimes call "positive liberty," and that we more commonly call self-government.[10] We care about democracy, in short, because we care about people governing themselves.

---

[10] "Negative" liberty consists in the absence of external social interference with one's chosen activities ("social," because gravity, e.g., doesn't count as an infringement of your negative liberty to fly), while "positive" liberty consists in social conditions allowing for effective exercise of one's faculties of judgment and choice in the giving of direction to one's life. The "negative"/"positive" distinction was apparently coined by Isaiah Berlin, "Two Concepts of Liberty,"

If so, then a political arrangement is defective if it fails to serve the people's self-government in roughly the way that democracy, according to some theory, is supposed to serve it.[11] Consider, for example, this account of how democracy serves self-government, on which we'll see Professors Post and Dworkin converging from their opposite-looking initial conceptions: Democracy serves self-government by providing each individual with a reason to identify his or her political will or "agency" with the lawmaking and other acts of collective institutions, or to claim such acts as his or her own. (In a philosophical usage, to speak of a person's or group's "agency" is to make reference to his or her or its faculty of taking action, of intentionally deciding and then doing something. "Agency" in that sense will be a handy term for us to have available here.)

In the views of both Post and Dworkin, as well as in Justice Brennan's and my own, the reference to individuals is crucial.[12] For to say that we value democracy for the sake of self-government is not yet to say who or what is the agent or subject of the self-government we have in mind—who or what is the self whose government by him of himself, or by her of herself, or by it of

---

in Berlin, *Four Essays on Liberty* (Oxford: Oxford University Press, 1969), 118–72. Compare Benjamin Constant's earlier distinction between the "liberties of the ancients" (= "positive") and the "liberties of the moderns" (= "negative"). See Benjamin Constant, "The Liberties of the Ancients Compared With the Liberties of the Moderns," in Constant, *Political Writings*, ed. Biancamaria Fontana (Cambridge: Cambridge University Press, 1988), 308–28. Charles Taylor, "What's Wrong with Negative Liberty?" in Taylor, *Philosophy and the Human Science (Philosophical Papers 2)* (Cambridge: Cambridge University Press, 1985), 211–29.

[11] Both Professors Dworkin and Post share this view. See, e.g., Robert Post, *Constitutional Domains: Democracy, Community, Management* (Cambridge, Mass.: Harvard University Press, 1995), 273, 278, 283–84; Ronald Dworkin, *Freedom's Law: The Moral Reading of the American Constitution* (Cambridge, Mass.: Harvard University Press, 1996), 21–22. Even while echoing Isaiah Berlin's famous warning against confusion of the human goods of positive and negative liberty (see id. chap. 8), Dworkin does plainly hold self-government to be a very important human good.

[12] As to Justice Brennan, see chapter 2.

itself, is the self-government we care about. American constitutional theorists often like to speak and write as if the agent in question is the capital-P People of the country somehow taken whole, as one, unified self. That, of course, implies that democracy's point is to give effect to a single political will attributed to a single popular agent—a will that has by some means, typically involving a majority vote or a series of them, earned the right to speak in the name of the People.[13]

I am betting, though, that that is not how you, Reader, in all innocence and candor see the matter, and in fact it's hard to imagine that most Americans do. I am betting that for you, as for us (Brennan, Dworkin, Post, and me), what finally, morally matters here (assuming self-government matters to you at all) can only be the self-government—the freedom, the dignity—of persons. It's not that I think you doubt that there really are in the world such things to speak of as nations and peoples and political communities, or that there are reasons to care about the histories and fates and flourishings and even in some sense the freedoms of these entities. None of us doubts that.[14] It is, however, entirely another question whether a group or community can be a subject or agent of self-government. Self-government, I take it—the state of living a life of one's own under one's own direction—is a human good in its own right; certainly not the only human good, maybe hard to defend as the chief human good, but still a human good that is not paltry, and one that it does not seem that a group or community can have.

Not, at any rate, unless you can grasp—and I am betting that you can't, any more than I can—how the distinct human good of

---

[13] The most sophisticated theorist at work today on how this right is earned is Bruce Ackerman. See his *We the People: Foundations* (Cambridge, Mass.: Harvard University Press, 1991); *We The People: Transformations* (Cambridge, Mass.: Harvard University Press, 1998).

[14] For the agreements of Professors Dworkin and Post, see below, pp. 30–31 and Frank I. Michelman, "Must Constitutional Democracy Be 'Responsive'?" *Ethics* 107 (July 1997): 706–23, pp. 710–12. Regarding Justice Brennan, see chapter 2, below, pp. 113–19.

being a self-governing subject can accrue to anyone or anything that, try as you and I might, we cannot see as having a consciousness and a will of its own. We do not understand a nation or a people or a political community to be a being possessed of its own mind, its own ability to feel or experience or decide—possessed, in other words, of a capacity for self-directive agency for which we have any final, moral reason to care. I know of nothing to suggest that Brennan believed *that*, any more than, I am sure, Professors Post or Dworkin believe it.[15] Any loose talk in these pages of a country's people governing themselves must, therefore, be taken to refer to the self-government of "everyone," meaning of and by each person.

The Institutional Difficulty

No doubt, such an individualistic notion of "everyone's" political self-government is beset with severe problems. Perhaps (it's controversial among both social and psychiatric theorists) individuals can be more or less self-governing in some departments of life. But try to explain how everyone can conceivably be self-governing on the field of politics, where laws are made. Laws can, of course, in some countries at some times, be made by the actions of individuals, those we would call autocratic rulers. In no country at any time, however, can *everyone* thus make the laws.

The creation of laws is irreducibly a social and collective activity in two, crucial respects. First, what is created as law for one must serve as law for all. True, a law can, in a sense, *apply to* a single person—as would, for example, a law made by autocrat Jones giving Jones a special and unique privilege of taking whatever he wants from anyone. But that law is a law *for* everyone; otherwise, there would be no point in calling it a law. (Try re-

---

[15] Cf. Post, *Constitutional Domains* 306 ("Groups neither reason nor have an autonomous will; only persons do.") As for Dworkin, see below, pp. 30–31. For Brennan, see chapter 2.

sisting Jones trying to take something from you, and you wind up in court.) Second, no prescription will actually work as a law—people won't recognize and comply with it as such—unless there is a sufficient base of social agreement on the authority to make laws of whoever issued the prescription. When dictator Jones gives out with the Jones law, either folks credit what he says as really making a law or they don't. If they don't, no law is made. If they do, then Jones making the law is functioning as a lawmaking *official* or *institution* in his society.

Officials and institutions are social creations. So are customs, and all law-creation is accomplished by either some institutional or some customary means. Customary law is an accretion over time of the uncodified habits, norms, and expectations of successive, socially dominant fractions of a country's population. Official-made law may be a product of the dictatorship of a ruler or ruling group, or it may be a product of deliberation and voting among those subject to the laws, or their representatives. All these modes of law creation are social to the core, and there would appear to be no other way for lawmaking to happen.

Democracy surely means that we do it by discussions leading up to votes in which everyone gets to participate on an equal footing with everyone else. But all real-world votes have losers, and none is ever decided by the sole and independent action of any individual. So the questions are: How is everyone to regard himself or herself as self-governing through social and institutional transactions from which many have dissented and in which in any event there is no real chance that any single person's own vote, or speech, or other considered political action decided the outcome? How is a person self-governing through institutional creation of laws that are revolting to him or her? (I'm sure you can think of some laws in force where you are that are revolting to you.)

Viewing matters from the standpoint of a concern about individual self-government in politically decidable matters, this is what we may call the Institutional Difficulty. The activity of a judge like Brennan is an example or an instance of the Institutional Difficulty, for such judges do indeed, as we'll soon see, create laws that are binding on you and me. (They do it by what we call "interpretation" of legal texts and precedents.) However, the law-creative activities of the Brennans is certainly not the *cause* of the Difficulty. The cause of the Difficulty is the simple, irremediable fact that *someone* has to make the laws, and we can't all do it for ourselves individually.

Interestingly, far from someone like Brennan being a cause of the Institutional Difficulty, both Professor Post and Professor Dworkin think he is or might be a part of its cure. How so? Both Post and Dworkin say that *democracy*, when rightly understood and carried out, can provide a warrant in reason for every individual's identification of his or her political agency with the collective acts of lawmaking institutions. If that is true, our Brennans might indeed play a crucial part in securing the possibility of individual self-government in and through democratic politics. The Brennans, then, might use their judicial powers of oversight of ordinary lawmaking to help ensure that democracy is, in practice, understood and carried out in the way that does make it a medium of the self-government of individuals.

So say our authors. Let us see.

THE SUBSTANTIVE CONCEPTION
OF DEMOCRACY

Substance and Procedure

Social and legal theorists sometimes use the term "social norm" to encompass various prescriptive propositions that we more commonly would call moral and legal rules, standards, principles, and judgments. Social norms can be extremely abstract and general (the Golden Rule), or extremely specific and concrete (1998 Iowa State Fair blue ribbon for cucurbits rightly belongs to that 300-pound cuke right over there), or anywhere in between. Legal theorists further make use of a distinction between "substantive" (or "primary") norms and "procedural" (or "secondary") norms. Roughly, a substantive or primary social norm does, and a procedural or secondary norm does not, contain information about what rights and obligations people are supposed to have, or, in other words, about how people in various social settings ought and ought not to act in regard to each other's interests and claims. But don't all social norms, by definition, contain information of that kind? According to the substance/procedure distinction, some do not. Some norms, it is said—the secondary, procedural ones—are directed only to the question of the method or procedure to be used in deciding the content of the substantive (primary) norms. Thus, "The legislature votes on it" is the secondary or procedural norm and "don't possess cannabis" is the resulting primary or substantive norm; "spin the bottle" is the secondary or procedural norm and "kiss *him*" (*he* being the one the bottle points to, the bottle having been duly spun) is the resulting primary or substantive norm.

Dworkin's Conception of Democracy as (the Right) Rights

"Democratic" is the name of a norm or standard (or maybe more than one) meant for application to political arrangements and practices; some are, some aren't, and we apply the standard in deciding which is which. According to Dworkin, the standard "democratic," as meant for application to a country's basic laws, is best conceived as a cluster of primary, substantive requirements, not of secondary, procedural ones. In Dworkin's view, the question of the democratic credentials of the basic laws of a country is best conceived as one of matter not manner. It is the newsperson's "what" that counts here, not the who, when, where, or how. In other words: To find out whether democracy prevails in a country on the level of its basic laws, you do not ask how or when or by whom those laws were made, you ask what those laws say.

Depending on what rights they establish, a country's basic laws may or may not serve democratic ends and values. They do so, in Dworkin's view, insofar as they rule out caste, guarantee a broad and equitable political franchise, prevent arbitrary legal discriminations and other oppressive uses of state powers, and assure governmental respect for freedoms of thought, expression, and association and for the intellectual and moral independence of every citizen.[16]

As we are going to see repeatedly below, "basic laws" here has to include not only the clauses of the Constitution but key interpretations of them. For example, the Equal Protection Clause in our Constitution does not necessarily or unqualifiedly count in Dworkin's eyes as a democratic feature in our system of government. It did not serve as such when construed as the Supreme Court construed it in *Plessy v. Ferguson* (1896) to permit states to segregate people by race into "separate but equal" public facilities. It did when the Court construed it in *Brown v. Board of Education* (1954) and succeeding cases to prohibit states from doing just that. Few would dispute these particular judgments. But judgments of the democratic or democracy-serving character of constitutional interpretations can be and often are very controversial. For example, many Americans find that the Equal Protection Clause stands in democracy's way when construed to prohibit race-conscious government action in the contemporary United States—whereas, needless to say, quite a few other people think exactly the opposite. That is why, if we accept Dworkin's view, a commitment to democracy on the basic-law level has to mean a striving not only to get the right abstract principles written into clauses of the Constitution but also to get key interpretations of those clauses—does "equal protection" mean that affirmative action is permitted or that it is not?—resolved in accord with the right or best conception of a democratic regime.

[16] See Dworkin, *Freedom's Law*, 16–18, 24–26; Ronald Dworkin, "Equality, Democracy, and Constitution: We the People in Court," *Alberta Law Review* 28 (1990): 324–46.

From Democracy-as-Rights to the Democratic Vindication of Judicial Governance: Alleged Institutional Advantages of the Judiciary

If you grant that much, Dworkin immediately goes on to point out, you must admit that there is nothing necessarily anti-democratic about allowing the country to be fundamentally governed, in part, by judges interpreting the basic laws. You have accepted that the objective for democracy, at the basic-law level, is not only to proclaim as law the right abstract principles but also to arrive at interpretations of them reflecting the right or best conception of a democratic regime. So it must be your view that there is in fact such a thing to speak of as the right or best conception of a democratic regime. It must, in other words, be your view that when people disagree about what the right or best conception is and about which interpretation of an abstract constitutional clause the right or best conception calls for, it's not just a matter of *chacun à son goût* but rather a matter of one party's getting closer than the other to the truth. But then, runs the line of Dworkin's thought, you have to admit the practical possibility that an independent judiciary will tend to get closer to the truth than would the great body of the people or their elected tribunes in the legislatures.[17]

Here, Dworkin's argument implicitly ties into a body of American legal and constitutional thought—sometimes called "legal process"—that is concerned with the relative strengths and weaknesses of different branches of government in the making of various kinds of decisions. Unpacked, this stage of the argument might run as follows.

American constitutionalism subordinates the ordinary lawmaking powers of any sitting government to the constraint of superior laws of lawmaking. An inevitable accompaniment of any such arrangement is that disagreements sometimes break out over whether the government, by its making of some ordinary law (or

---

[17] See Dworkin, *Freedom's Law*, 32–35.

its failure to make one), remains in compliance with the superior law, and there have to be ways of getting those disagreements officially resolved so that life may go on.[18]

In the established constitutional practice of our country, many such disagreements are referred for official resolution to the law courts and particularly the Supreme Court of the United States. There is an obvious connection between that fact and the fact that the Supreme Court heads up what we call an "independent" judiciary, meaning primarily one whose members, once chosen, are not beholden either to the voters or to elected officials for retention of their positions or their salaries.[19] The Court is in that sense outside the sitting government that stands charged with illegal lawmaking, and there is apparent good reason to send the charges of illegal action to an outside body for decision. Wouldn't it be both morally and prudentially reckless to leave them for decision by the accused government itself? To do so, Professor Dworkin has written, would be contrary to "the principle that no

[18] Dispute over the constitutionality of the government's *failure* to make a law is largely foreign to American experience, but is much more familiar in some other countries. South Africa's constitution, for instance, requires the country's elected Parliament to enact and keep in force legislation "to prevent or prohibit unfair discrimination." Constitution of South Africa, 1996, §9(4). Since the concept of "unfair discrimination" is obviously one that is subject to sincere political debate and disagreement, it is easy to imagine questions arising, which some official institution will have to answer, over whether Parliament is duly performing its constitutional obligation. It looks as though that task will fall mainly to the Constitutional Court of South Africa.

One might ask why the authors of a constitution don't just include in the instrument itself the law against "unfair discrimination" (or whatever) that they are evidently ready to maintain is morally or prudentially required of the governmental system they are chartering. The most likely answers are either *(i)* the constitutional authors believe for some reason that they are not in the best situation to write the morally or prudentially requisite antidiscrimination law in full detail, or *(ii)* although they agree on the abstract principle of having a law against unfair discrimination, they can't agree on what the details of such a law should be, and they don't want to risk the political success of their constitution-making project as a whole on a full airing of their disagreement.

[19] By command of Article III of the Constitution, federal judges are presidential appointees (subject to Senate confirmation) and have life tenure, and judicial salaries may be increased from time to time, but never reduced.

man should be judge in his own cause."[20] Others speak of setting the fox to guard the chickens.

But that's not enough to close the case in favor of giving un-elected judges the decisive word on these questions of the higher, constitutional legality of ordinary lawmakings. To be sure, we may want a decider who stands outside the accused government, but the courts are not the only such decider available. Another is the body of the country's people, the sitting government's sup-posed bosses. It would seem that, on strict democratic principle, the entitlement to pass on questions of the higher legality of ordi-nary lawmakings belongs by right to this body. Disputes about the higher legality of particular instances of ordinary lawmaking are nothing other than disputes about how to apply the laws of lawmaking and questions about how to apply the laws of law-making are not cleanly separable from questions about what the laws of lawmaking *are*. Acts of legal application contain acts of legal manufacture. Consider the Supreme Court deciding for the first time, over intense and reasonable disagreement, that the Equal Protection Clause very strictly limits governmental use of affirmative action. In what sense is the Court not engaged in the making of a law of lawmaking? As we'll see below, there are many such cases—cases in which you cannot apply the laws of law-making without, at the same time, in some nontrivial measure, making them. But by the principle of democracy, it is the people of a country who are entitled to be the makers of the basic laws of that country.

If it were beyond imagining how we could practically arrange for the people to have a deciding voice in constitutional interpre-tation, we might shrug the problem off on that ground. However, it is not. A simple way to do it is to abolish judicial review. If Congress or a state legislature stands charged with enacting laws that the laws of lawmaking prohibit, or with failing to enact laws that the laws of lawmaking command, let the voters decide

---

[20] Ronald Dworkin, "The Jurisprudence of Richard Nixon," *The New York Review of Books*, May 4, 1972.

the charges at the next elections. They can find out how candi-
dates stand on the matter and elect those who will carry out
the people's judgment, repealing the offending law or enacting
the missing one. Congress then is not the judge of its own
cause, or a fox set to guard the people's chickens. Congress may
have a cause, but the people are the judge; Congress may be a
fox, but the people are the guard. To make the Court the judge
and the guard is, from the standpoint of democracy, to put the
Court in the people's rightful place. So it might be and has been
contended.

If there is to be found a justification for setting the Court as
the guard, the form of it will have to be: the Court is an institution
much better situated and equipped to do a good job of it than
are either the people or their elected representatives in the
legislatures. As it happens, there is no shortage of impressive-
looking arguments to that effect. Many begin with the observa-
tion that what is at stake here is not *preference* but *judgment*, and
judgment, at that, of issues of a somewhat philosophical character,
such as which of the competing interpretations of some abstract
basic-law principle conforms to the right or best conception of a
democratic regime. It may not be a very good idea—assuming it
would be possible in practice—to turn every legislator's every
vote on a pending bill, and every citizen's every decision about
whom to vote for in a congressional or state legislative election,
into an occasion of judgment of such issues. They are issues to
which full-time political philosophers dedicate their lives, and to
impose them on legislators and citizens in their ordinary political
activities may be to overload those activities preposterously and
ruinously.

Legislators and citizens, it may be said, have too many other
things legitimately on their minds. Legislators considering bills
are legitimately concerned with public policy options to which
constitutional law and morality are indifferent (far from every
legislative policy choice is a matter of basic political morality),
and with constituent preferences about those policy options
(more guns? less butter? less bread? more circuses?). Constituents

selecting representatives are legitimately concerned with public policy choices, with expressions of preference as between policies of equal moral defensibility (that's democracy, too), and with the general honesty, wisdom, courage, and leadership of those running for office. So if ordinary political operations do inevitably engage questions of a political-philosophical character, about the morally necessary constraints on government, there may be good reasons for placing primary responsibility for dealing with those questions in an institution better designed for the purpose, and less preoccupied by other purposes, than an ordinary legislature or an ordinary electorate is, most of the time. Let the electorate and the legislatures act on the basis of policy and preference, and leave it to the judges to tell them when their policies and preferences are over the line of morally necessary constraint. Correlatively, choose judges with due regard for their fitness for this sort of work.

So it is often contended. The contention goes arm in arm with Dworkin's argument that investing the judiciary with final authority to say what abstract constitutional clauses more concretely mean is not counter-democratic "in principle," just as such, at least not once you grant that a commitment to democracy on the basic-law level means a striving not only to get the right abstract principles into the basic law but to get key interpretations of those principles resolved in accord with the right or best conception of a democratic regime.

A clear intention of Dworkin's argument is to provide a defense of Justice Brennan's career against charges of riding roughshod over democracy. Of course, it's not Brennan by name that Dworkin defends but the mode of constitutional adjudication that Brennan's career epitomizes. Assuming Brennan's constitutional interpretations match up well with what *you* think makes for a substantively democratic regime—the goods are on display in chapter 2—you should have no trouble counting him a historic contributor to the improvement of democracy in America.

Actually, matters aren't so simple for Professor Dworkin. For him, remember, a part of democracy's point is self-government, and it seems almost facetious to associate self-government with a notion of democracy's being a matter *only* of the substance or content of the basic laws and *not at all* a matter of who wrote those laws and by what procedures. Inescapably, "self-government" is the name of an activity, a reference to something that someone *does*. It would seem to follow that no simple test of outcomes on any given level of lawmaking, the constitutional level included, can reveal the presence or absence of self-government on that same level of lawmaking. From the standpoint of a concern about self-government, democracy is present only when a country's people decide for themselves, by democratic political procedures, all of those major conditions of their lives that are politically decidable at all. Insofar as those conditions include the contents of the country's basic laws (which they quite obviously do—I gave examples at the beginning of this chapter), a population's passive reception of those contents from judicial oracles must register as a serious shortfall from the democratic ideal.

But can that really be the right way to comprehend "democracy"? Can democracy conceivably mean that the people decide, democratically, *all* the politically decidable questions? Can a commitment to democracy really require the use of democratic procedures to decide even the basic laws of the country, including the rules and norms that set the aims and limits of governmental powers and establish the system for any and all further lawmaking? Daunting though it may be, the answer seems to be "yes," in view of the moral and material importance that people quite reasonably attach to the contents of many of these basic laws, these laws of lawmaking. And yet I suspect we will always feel (as I would guess many readers are feeling right now) an impulse to exclude the laws *of lawmaking* from democracy's procedural purview—to restrict the domain of procedurally democratic decision to whatever *further* political choices the laws of lawmaking leave open, while leaving *those* laws to be decided by right and true reasoning about what it means for a lawmaking system to be democratic.

Exactly this impulse to exclude the laws of lawmaking from the domain of decision by democratic procedures is what we see exemplified in Dworkin's proposal that we judge the democratic credentials of a constitution by reference to its content and not by reference to its authorship. This impulse to exclude is irrepressible. It is irrepressible for a reason. The reason is that behind the impulse there stands an apparently crushing logical objection to the alternative idea, that the contents of the laws of lawmaking could, consistently with a commitment to democratic government, themselves be within the keeping of a democratic procedure to decide. We take a close look at that objection below, but first we need to notice how another factor might independently lead Professor Dworkin to seek the American Constitution's democratic credentials in its regulative content and not in the procedures used to create that content.

Interpretation (I): "Moral Reading" versus Procedural Legitimation

Textbook theory typically takes an opposite tack from Dworkin's. It tries to uphold the Constitution's democratic credentials in strictly procedural terms, by picturing the country's people, acting wholly or partly through votes cast by elected representatives, as having indeed chosen the laws of lawmaking for themselves. The simple version is that they did so on the various occasions when conventions in the original states ratified the original Constitution, when state legislatures or conventions ratified its several amendments, and when conventions in territories petitioning for statehood ratified (in effect) the constitution as then amended. Much more refined and complex versions are also in circulation.[21] One could cite a number of grounds for

---

[21] See Bruce Ackerman, *We the People: Foundations* (Cambridge, Mass.: Harvard University Press, 1993); Bruce Ackerman, *We the People: Transformations* (Cambridge, Mass.: Harvard University Press, 1998).

doubting the cogency and credibility of claims of this sort,[22] but here I only want to make the point that it is closed off to Dworkin because of a view he holds about what judges really do when they interpret laws in the course of deciding how to apply the laws to cases.

At the point of application to cases, constitutional law is always a product of someone's interpretation of the constitutional clauses, judicial precedents and doctrines, and lawyers' conventional understandings of which this law is formed. So argues Dworkin, and I agree, and perhaps most lawyers would. But Dworkin carries the point to lengths where not everyone would follow, although I do. He finds no escape from what he calls a "moral reading" of certain clauses of the Constitution that appear to confer rights in very abstract terms, including those which speak of "the freedom of speech," "liberty," "due process of law," and "equal protection of the law." A legal interpreter of these expressions, Dworkin says, has no choice but to treat them as "invocations" of political-moral values or principles that the interpreter has the responsibility to distill from what he or she finds to be major fixed points in the historical practice of American constitutionalism. Such a distillation, Dworkin maintains, simply cannot be accomplished without putting into the brew some of the interpreter's own substantive vision of the proper ends and ideals of government.[23]

We can use an opinion of Justice Brennan's to illustrate the moral reading approach to constitutional interpretation. The case of *Michael H. v. Gerald D.* (1989)[24] concerned an unwedded man in California who sought a right to visitation with a child he had fathered, whose mother was married to another man at the time

[22] Many are set forth in Ronald Dworkin, *A Matter of Principle* (Cambridge, Mass.: Harvard University Press, 1985), 33–71. See also Frank I. Michelman, "Constitutional Authorship," in Larry Alexander, ed., *Constitutionalism: Philosophical Foundations* (Cambridge: Cambridge University Press, 1998), 64–98.

[23] See, e.g., Dworkin, *Freedom's Law*, 2–4.

[24] 491 U.S. 110 (1989).

when the child was born. California law, like the laws of other states, had long denied the biological father any right of visitation in these circumstances. It declared the person to whom the mother was married at childbirth to be the legal father, making the other man, in the sight of the law, a stranger to the family. Michael H. sought relief from this law, claiming that his interest in contact with his biological child is a constitutionally protected component of the liberty protected by the Fourteenth Amendment. Justice Antonin Scalia, writing for a majority of the Supreme Court said it can't be that because American law typically and traditionally had never granted visitation rights to men in Michael's position.[25] Brennan, dissenting, protested against this method of decision. He recalled prior Court decisions extending the protection of the Amendment's "liberty" clause to a class of what he called "generalized interests" that "society traditionally has thought important." Among these generalized interests, Brennan listed "freedom from physical restraint, marriage, childbearing, [and] childrearing."[26] He said the decisive question must be whether the biological father's visitation interest falls in all reason under an even more general principle of liberty that these traditionally esteemed, generalized interests exemplify. In Brennan's view, the law's preexistent refusal to respond to a biological father's visitation interest might have to be judged a failure on the law's part to measure up to its own immanent standard of reason and right. Correcting for such failures was, in Brennan's view, a chief mission of the office he held.

Nothing could better exemplify what Dworkin commends as a "moral reading" of the Constitution. But, as the case also illustrates and Dworkin explicitly recognizes, to give a moral reading to constitutional clauses and precedents often means to take sides on some matter of political-moral controversy on which sincere and thoughtful people can and do differ. "Intractable, profound

---

[25] See ibid., 124.
[26] Ibid., 136, 139 (Brennan, J., dissenting).

questions of political morality," Dworkin has called them, that
"philosophers, statesmen, and citizens have debated for many
centuries with no prospect of agreement."[27] I mentioned examples of such issues near the beginning of this chapter. Notions of
equality and democracy, freedom and fairness, can doubtless help
frame debate over them, but the sincerest commitment to such
ideals cannot incontrovertibly settle them. Such a possibility is
precluded by diversities of experience and vision and the thousand
shocks to which human judgment is heir. In the face of resulting,
unliquidatable, reasonable disagreement, someone has to decide
these morally freighted questions of constitutional meaning, and
whoever, for whatever reason, is excluded from participation in
the decision is to that extent fundamentally governed by those
who make it.

It should now be apparent why the moral reading theory of
constitutional interpretation debars its partisans from the procedural way of defending the democratic character of judicially interpreted constitutional law—that is, by pointing to historical
facts of popular enactment of the constitutional clauses that the
judges interpret. On the moral reading theory, those popularly
enacted clauses contain too small a share, and the judicial interpretations of them too large a share, of the total sum of operative
constitutional meaning that is to be made. Too much meaning
remains open at the point of promulgation and ratification of the
constitutional text by popular forces. Insofar as democracy is
about self-government, democracy means the people deciding for
themselves, by political procedures, the politically decidable conditions of social life in which they have moral or material reason
to take an interest. It follows that, if someone is going to use
"moral readings" of highly interpretable constitutional texts to
resolve for the country such basic and contested issues of political
morality and prudence as those presented by affirmative action,
racist speech, gay rights, property rights (e.g., as against environmental regulation), political campaign finance, term limits for

---

[27] Dworkin, *Life's Dominion*, 120.

elected officeholders, assisted suicide, abortion, etc. (the list is end-less), it ought to be the people acting democratically who do that and not any cadre of independent judges. Work of that sort simply cannot be placed beyond democracy's purview, given a conception of democracy's point in which self-government strongly figures.[28]

Nevertheless, it may have to, for the story is not over yet.

[28] I expect some resistance to this conclusion, although not much from Profes-sor Dworkin, so I want at least to indicate briefly how I would go about heading off what I think are the three likeliest lines of objection to it, which I will call the objections from abstraction, from concretion, and from right-answerism.

Here is a schematic rendition of the objection from abstraction: It should not be insuperably difficult for a constitutional interpreter to arrive at, and publicly defend, a determination of whether the people have or have not ever politically enacted into their constitutional instrument an expression of the principle of (for example) equality of political concern and respect. Suppose the answer is that they have. Then to that extent the question of the people's self-government depends strictly on whether the government they receive back from judges and others does or does not thereafter proceed in true accord with the principle of political equality that the people themselves enacted. As long as it does, all is well; the people govern themselves.

I don't believe it. It appears to me that self-government is too gravely compro-mised by the range and gravity of the questions that the abstract principle of political equality leaves open to further debate and resolution. Only think of current controversy in America over governmental "colorblindness" as an un-compromisable principle of constitutional law. Issues of this magnitude are too fraught with moral and material significance to allow us to say that constitutional law is democratic in virtue of the people themselves having written the equal protection or due process clause into the Constitution.

But a principle of political equality (to continue with the example) is surely not the only one that the people may defensibly be found to have enacted into their governing instrument, which brings us to the objection from concretion or, as it might be called, the objection from integrity, which roughly is: The question for a constitutional interpreter is always one of how best to make an applicable synthesis of *numerous* abstract principles that the people over time have enacted into their constitution, adding into the normative mix whatever past synthetic interpretations have proven themselves to be enduring ones, and this is a far more thickly informed and constrained exercise than determining the application of any single abstract principle taken timelessly and alone. True enough. But not constraining enough to abate the problem I am posing. Dwor-kin himself has characterized these synthetic normative judgments of legal inter-pretation as both bottomlessly political and as having components of aesthetic judgment. See Dworkin, *Law's Empire*, 73–76, 87–93, 229–32. These seem to be ways of saying what I take to be true: that among sincere and reasonable

Dworkin's Account of Political Agency

Remember the Institutional Difficulty: How might a person be self-governing through institutional enactment of a law to which he is opposed? (Why not rather say that restrictions on majoritarian lawmaking in favor of individual liberty obviously support personal self-government?)[29]

Professor Dworkin says there is only one agent in sight that can honestly be seen to be making the laws, namely, the collective agent that we call a people or a citizenry. Therefore, he continues, the individual's ability to identify his own agency with the collective agent's lawmaking activity would be the only way in which there could possibly be satisfaction of each individual's interest in being a self-governing person. A solution to the Institutional Difficulty would depend, then, on the following sort of possibility: Observing a surrounding political community making laws through majoritarian political processes, a person can, by counting herself a member of that community, claim ownership of its lawmaking acts, can regard its acts as her own acts.[30]

Professor Dworkin proceeds to state certain rational preconditions for this sort of identification. You cannot, he says, reasonably ally your political agency with that of any collective body that does not by its actions maintain a due respect for your own

---

disputants, there are bound to be a plurality of constructions of the data—a duck perceived here, a rabbit perceived there; a social-realist tragedy here, a playful *roman à clef* there—that leave hanging in dispute the sorts of morally and materially freighted issues that people cannot leave to be resolved by others while seriously claiming to be governing themselves.

Which brings us to the objection from right-answerism. It may be said that the real-time interminable disputability of issues of constitutional interpretation does not mean there is no such thing as getting them right. That premise I accept without reservation. From it, someone might argue further that therefore people are self-governing as long as they enact the grist of the principles that go into an interpretation mill that is itself as aptly designed as we can make it to turn out true interpretations of the principles. My complex response to this claim appears in later sections of this chapter.

[29] See Dworkin, *Freedom's Law*, 21.

[30] Ibid., 21–22.

moral and intellectual singularity, and for the interest you accordingly take in both the contents of collective outcomes and your
capacities to influence them. What's required, then, is the collective's assurance to each member of: (1) unhindered and equal access to wide-open and effective channels of public-opinion formation; (2) an equal measure of consideration for the interests of
each in decisions of public policy; and (3) insulation from collective control of each individual's capacities for self-responsible
moral and intellectual reflection and judgment. Dworkin calls
these the "relational conditions" of "moral membership" in a political collectivity.[31] His list of relational conditions looks a lot
like what is guaranteed by our Constitution's First, Fifth, and
Fourteenth Amendments. Or, rather, to speak more finely, it
looks like what is found in those texts by certain moral readers of
them, like Brennan. Professor Dworkin meant precisely that it
should. His claim is that an independent judiciary can, by rightly
construing and effectuating constitutional law, secure fulfillment
of certain rational preconditions for an individual's identifying
his or her political agency with the lawmaking acts of his or her
political community. By thus securing the possibility of everyone's self-government on the field of lawmaking, the practice of
judicial review can, if well conducted, solve the Institutional Difficulty. Eureka!

A stunning argument, but I do not see how it can succeed. Professor Dworkin says that certain constitutional guarantees give
you a warrant in reason for a certain kind of identification of the
self with certain political events. That identification must reside
in your consciousness, as either a belief or a feeling. Say it is a
belief. What belief? Not the belief that you, the individual, actually make the laws or exert detectible influence on legislative outcomes, because one of Dworkin's starting points for this whole
discussion is that no one in large-scale democratic conditions can
reasonably believe that. Alternatively, you might believe that
sound judicial enforcement of the bill of rights and the rest of the

[31] Ibid., 24–26.

Constitution gives you reason to abide by the (other, further) laws that are collectively made. That sort of belief is not, however, sufficient to Dworkin's purpose. It would leave us with an account of how you might reasonably come to respect and accept laws made by some agency other than yourself, which is not at all the same thing as an account of how you might reasonably come to regard yourself as lawmaker to yourself.

Say, then, that it's not a belief that Dworkin has in mind, but a feeling. What feeling? Say it is a feeling of satisfaction or even pride that you take in lawmaking that is done by an organization that treats you and your independence and your interests with the kind of respect that is due to a member. Or even say it is a feeling, engendered by such treatment, that you did the lawmaking. Neither of those feelings is the same thing as your having done the lawmaking. Feeling is not doing, and for you to "identify" sympathetically with the doer of an act is not for you to have done the act. Dworkin seems to have mistaken a question about what a person has done for a question of what a person thinks, or how a person feels, about what someone else has done.[32]

On the face of it, Dworkin's message is a happy one. It offers resolution of an apparent contradiction between two of our deepest (professed) political desires—for a government of laws, for self-government. His argument seems meant to reassure and persuade us that we really can reconcile a democratic aspiration to political self-government *by everyone* with the practice of letting a few judges decide the applied contents of the country's basic laws. But I think the real, darker-hued, message is that there is no such reconciliation to be had. And this brings us back at last to the crushing logical objection I mentioned before, against the very idea that the contents of the laws of lawmaking could themselves be within the keeping of a democratic procedure to decide.

---

[32] For further exchange on this point between Professor Dworkin and the author, see Professor Dworkin's Comment on my original Lecture, Ronald Dworkin, "The Partnership Conception of Democracy," *California Law Review* 86 (1998): 453, and my response, Frank I. Michelman, "Rejoinders," *California Law Review* 86 (1998): 469, 475–77.

A PARADOX OF DEMOCRATIC COMMITMENT

If you really care about democracy, if democracy is a burning issue for you, *you have to mean something by it.* Your commitment to democracy means that you want your country's laws of lawmaking—as interpreted, as applied—to conform to the requirements of whatever it is that you do mean by "democracy."

Democracy, it appears, is a demanding normative idea, an idea with content, however uncertain or disputable its content may be. Maybe everyone agrees that democracy connotes a procedure of joint decision by lots of persons somehow acting together. But no less certainly does it connote a socially constituted relationship among parties to the procedure. We ought not, as Dworkin rightly insists, to regard a political decision procedure as democratic unless participants enter the procedure in the appropriate relations of equality, independence, freedom, and security, vis-à-vis one another and vis-à-vis the political collective and its powers. But then democracy requires—this is what I take Dworkin's darker-hued message to be—a kind of pre-inscription into the basic laws of a country of whatever constraints on subsequent political action are required to secure and maintain those democracy-constituting relations of equality, independence, freedom, and security. The ideal content of that requisite pre-inscription is not fluid or politically up for grabs. It is what it is, fixed by the notion of democracy that we hold and consider to be worth fighting for. Whether the ideal is at any moment satisfied or flouted is not, therefore, a question whose answer can ever be equated with the outcome of any vote or other collective decision procedure, every single one of which carries some liability to get things wrong.

I can imagine someone answering: "Enough with these failures of nerve, these flights from *real* democratic conviction. What *I* mean by democracy is a commitment, come what may and for better or worse, to letting all public questions, including the question of what features in a social decision procedure qualify it as democratic, be decided by democratic procedures." But you would be speaking nonsense if you said that. How could you possibly—how could you conceivably—contrive to have democracy decide the question of what democracy means or requires in the first place? In order to judge that it was indeed a democratic procedure to which you were submitting the question of democracy's requirements, you would have to know the answer to the question you were submitting before you submitted it. It absolutely is not possible to appoint democracy to decide what democracy is.[33]

It is necessity, then, that explains the irrepressible impulse to exclude basic-law determinations from the procedural purview of democracy. This impulse does not ultimately spring from reflection on what it is prudent or desirable to give to democracy to do. Rather, it springs from logic. This logic, unhappily for some, apparently bars democracy from a decision-space where it would seem urgently and rightly to want to go, that of deciding the contents of the most basic of a dedicatedly democratic country's laws, its laws of lawmaking. The paradox of democracy is now in full bloom.

THE PROCEDURAL CONCEPTION
OF DEMOCRACY

Is there some way to refurbish our sense of the logical possibility of using democratic procedures to decide even the most basic of a dedicatedly democratic country's laws? It is with this question in mind that I now turn us toward the "responsive democracy" theory of Robert Post.

Recall our two leading questions. First: how might one simultaneously embrace both democracy and the judicial activism of a

---

[33] As Professor Dworkin has said, democracy "cannot prescribe the procedures for testing whether the conditions for the procedures it does prescribe are met." Dworkin, *Freedom's Law*, 33.

constitutional judge like Brennan? Second: how might a person be considered self-governing through political enactment of a law to which he is opposed? Remember also the form of the answers that I said would be posed by both Professors Post and Dworkin: Brennan may be a hero of both democracy and self-government. It may be that he as a judge was uniquely well situated to ensure the effectuation by law of certain principles that, when honored, can turn majoritarian political institutions into vehicles of everyone's self-government. For Professor Dworkin following that line of thought, democracy on the level of the basic laws is, as we have seen, a strictly substantive standard—but one that seems, as such, to be achingly incomplete. For Professor Post following that line of thought, democracy on the level of the basic laws is, as we are about to see, a procedural standard—but one that turns out, in spite of good intentions, to be hooked on substance.

Post's Account of Political Agency: "Responsive Democracy"

For liberals who care about individual self-government, the obvious problem of politics is that pure self-determination by everyone in politically decidable matters, such as what the laws shall provide, is unattainable in a world where deep divisions of opinion preclude consensus on each and every major question of social ordering. Robert Post envisions, as the best available substitute for the lawmaking consensus that we cannot have, a legally guaranteed access for everyone, absolutely equally and unrestrictedly, to a continuing forum in which individuals contribute vectors of opinion and preference to periodic summations that decide, for the time being, the public regulations of social life. Post calls this process "public discourse." It can occur wherever in modern society political and cultural exchanges occur: in public meetings, in cyberspace, in classrooms, on streets, and—overwhelmingly—in what we call the media. Post uses the term "responsive democracy" to signify the way in which a political system built around

an uncompromising commitment to radically free public discourse can provide for everyone's self-government.[34] He aims to
show how it is thereby possible

> to reconcile individual autonomy with collective self-deter-
> mination by subordinating governmental decision-making
> to communicative processes sufficient to instill in citizens a
> sense of participation, legitimacy, and identification. Al-
> though . . . there may be no determinative fusion of individ-
> ual and collective will, citizens can . . . embrace the govern-
> ment as rightfully "their own" because of engagement in
> these communicative processes.

Who or what is responsive democracy supposed to be responsive *to*? The answer is: to you and to me. The point is to maintain
a set of social and legal conditions in which each individual who
cares to exercises actual self-rule, not directly but by making in-
puts to the institutional events, and behind them to the cultural
shifts and flows, that continuingly shape and reshape what Post
calls the "national identity" and "social order."[35] By "social order,"
Post means mainly, if not only, the country's basic system of lawmaking institutions and practices that I have called the laws of
lawmaking. By "national identity," I take him to mean those aspects of a country's prevailing moral sensibilities, beliefs, and
concerns that find expression in the institutional basics of the social order and in the series of legal regulations of social life that
issue out of them. (An example would be a characteristic American attraction to self-reliance, competition, and rewards to merit.)
I take Post's claim to be roughly this: when a lawmaking system,
and the public values that supply it with direction and momen-
tum, are visibly and constantly being forged and tested in radically
free public discourse, then that lawmaking system is one with

---

[34] See generally Post, *Constitutional Domains*. I consider responsive democracy
theory at greater length in "Must Constitutional Democracy Be 'Responsive'?"
Ethics 107 (July 1997): 706–23.

[35] Post, *Constitutional Domains*, 275, 185.

which every inhabitant of the country can identify as an "owner," responsible as such for all the laws that the system makes from time to time.[36] The system and its resulting laws can then be said to have been freely chosen by everyone, at least in the sense that everyone can see the system as an authentic representation of the sum of the preferences and opinions that individuals have severally and freely contributed to the public-discourse melting-pot. So a chief practical aim of responsive democracy theory is to specify the social conditions, including the legal conditions, in which all individuals can have a warranted sense of autonomous and effective contribution, through public discourse, to the process of creating the social order in which they live.

Does all this sound a lot like Professor Dworkin describing the "relational conditions" of a person's moral membership in a political collective, which enable her to identify her agency with the collective's lawmaking?[37] I *said* they would meet up.

Among the requisite legal conditions, Post believes, is that we rigorously guarantee, by laws of lawmaking insofar as they can do it for us (Post has in mind the First Amendment, prohibiting laws that "abridge[ ] the freedom of speech, or of the press") a "structure of communication" that is always absolutely, unrestrictedly open to all views that anyone might hold regarding the national identity or social order.[38] As Post says, "If the state were to forbid the expression of a particular idea, the government would become, with respect to individuals holding that idea, heteronomous [i.e., a government of one person by other persons] and undemocratic."[39] But if, his argument runs, we maintain a reasonably capacious sphere of absolutely unrestricted public discourse, then the national identity that's constantly being hammered out in this public space can be said to be one that we, each and together, have freely made and chosen. Then and only then it may

---

[36] See ibid., 273, 311–12.
[37] See above, pp. 30–31.
[38] Post, *Constitutional Domains*, 185–86.
[39] Ibid., 304; see also 274.

be said that the legal regulations of social life that issue from and reflect this freely chosen national identity are consistent with self-determination.

Post's Pure-Proceduralist ("Anti-Foundationalist") Ambition

Recall our distinction between substantive and procedural social norms.[40] With clear purpose, Robert Post presents the theory of responsive democracy as positing only a procedural norm, as resting on no substantive "foundation" of (inevitably controversial) ideas about what is good for people, or about how they deserve or are entitled to be treated by one another, or about what (apart from the procedure by which it is reached) makes a political outcome a just or legitimate or otherwise desirable outcome. Recurring to the fine formulation of French political theorist Claude Lefort, Post speaks of democracy as "a regime founded upon the legitimacy of a debate as to what is legitimate and what is illegitimate—a debate which is necessarily without any guarantor and without any end."[41] In order for us to be truly self-governing, these words seem to say, the procedures of democratic decisionmaking cannot be limited by any norm or goal other than the formal requirement of the equal openness of the procedures themselves to all persons and all views.

You may already notice something puzzling here. Neither Post nor Lefort is quite claiming that democracy is whatever a democratic debate determines democracy to be. (How could anyone claim such a thing with even a shred of plausibility? What if a democratic debate decided that democracy means dictatorial rule by Fred Schauer?)[42] To put the same thought another way: Nei-

---

[40] See above, pp. 16–17.

[41] Post, *Constitutional Domains*, 23, 186, quoting Claude Lefort, *Democracy and Political Theory*, David Macey, trans. (Minneapolis: University of Minnesota Press, 1988), 39.

[42] It doesn't matter who Fred Schauer is, but I can tell you that the example is adapted from Frederick Schauer, "Amending the Presuppositions of a Consti-

ther Post nor Lefort really conceives of democracy as a regime floating free of any and all foundational principles. Rather, to use Lefort's exact terms, democracy is a regime that is "founded"—founded upon "the legitimacy of a debate." Presumably, an affair must have certain features in order to be a debate at all, and perhaps certain additional features to be a legitimate one. (Otherwise, everything that calls itself a debate would be a legitimate debate, and the words "legitimate" and "debate" in Lefort's sentence would be idle.) Whatever these normatively required features of democratically legitimating debate may be, they evidently do, in the view of Lefort and Post, provide a necessary "foundation" for a regime that claims to be legitimate by reason of being democratic.

In spite of all, Post—along with no few other democratic-liberal theorists of our age[43]—feels the urge to speak of a regime that is without foundations, and one can see what may be feeding the urge. Suppose we distinguish between "pure procedural" and "procedure-independent" standards of rightness for basic laws or laws of lawmaking. An example of a pure procedural standard is: "Basic laws are right when they represent accurately the summation of the duly expressed preferences or opinions of every affected person." An example of a procedure-independent standard is: "Basic laws are right when they express and further a moral mandate of equal respect and concern for every citizen."[44] Procla-

---

tution," in Sanford Levinson, ed., *Responding to Imperfection: The Theory and Practice of Constitutional Amendment* (Princeton: Princeton University Press, 1995), 146–61, at 152–53.

[43] See, e.g., Don Herzog, *Without Foundations: Justification in Political Theory* (Ithaca: Cornell University Press, 1985).

[44] My category of a "pure procedural standard" corresponds directly to the case of what John Rawls calls "pure" procedural justice, where justice or rightness is directly equated with performing the procedure and abiding by its outcome. My category of "procedure-independent standards" includes (although it is not limited to) Rawls's cases of "perfect" and "imperfect" procedural justice, because those are both cases in which the conception of rightness refers to outcomes (e.g., the same size piece of cake for both of us) and not to any procedure (you cut, I pick), even if commitment to the conception carries with it an obligation to use a certain procedure because of the procedure's known

mation of a procedure-independent standard of rightness for laws can easily strike us as deeply at odds with self-government. After all, if there is some requirement—any requirement—that *the content* of the laws has to satisfy in order for the laws to be right, then to that extent it is not rightfully up to any of us, much less all of us, to say what the laws shall and shall not be; and to that extent, therefore, we cannot be self-governing, at least not rightfully so. Or so it may seem.

Brennan and the Proceduralist Conception

We don't want to meander too far afield of Justice Brennan and his example. Therefore let us ask: How should admirers of Justice Brennan's judicial career respond to responsive democracy theory with its pure-proceduralist, "anti-foundationalist" ambition? I think Brennan's own response would have to have been "yes and no." Brennan's famously libertarian free-speech decisions—for example, those treating flag-burning as a form of speech that the First Amendment protects against governmental restriction—say yes to public discourse as a key to personal self-government through political democracy.[45] And practically everything else in his judicial product says no to anti-foundationalism.

That product is full of things that a radically procedural standard for the rightness of a political regime cannot hope to explain. At the core of Brennan's constitutional jurisprudence apparently stands the moral idea, one that he carried with him to the Supreme bench, of the inestimable value of the ever-redeemable dignity of the individual human being.[46] This, plainly, is an idea

---

superior propensity to arrive at the desired outcome. See John Rawls, *A Theory of Justice* (Cambridge, Mass.: Harvard University Press, 1971), 85–86.

[45] See below, pp. 69–70, 78–83. Brennan joined the opinion of the Court (per Rehnquist, C. J.) in Hustler Magazine v. Falwell, 485 U.S. 46 (1988), to which Professor Post accords a central place in his reading of our free-speech jurisprudence. See Post, *Constitutional Domains*, chap. 4.

[46] See chapter 2 for details. In a speech given before his nomination to the Supreme Court, Brennan described the American system as "based upon the dignity and inviolability of the individual soul." The speech was reprinted in the

about moral substance, not procedure. It is an idea about how persons are to be treated, not an idea about how publicly to decide how persons are to be treated.

The core idea of human dignity, in Brennan's hands, implies a set of basic human rights that are both full of content and strongly foundational, in the sense that due regard for them is prerequisite to the legitimacy of any and all political power. Most dramatically, this idea motivates Brennan's death-penalty jurisprudence.[47] Against the tide of a strengthening Supreme Court majority, Justice Brennan came and stuck to the view that the death penalty is in all possible applications unconstitutional, a violation of the Eighth Amendment's prohibition of "cruel and unusual punishments," for the reason that it contradicts the "intrinsic worth" of the person we kill and is "degrading to human dignity."[48]

The same core notion also obviously inspired many others of Brennan's interpretations of constitutional clauses, including his views that the Constitution, without specifically saying so, must mean to guarantee rights to individualized hearings to those asserting eligibility for government benefits;[49] must mean that government cannot wantonly denounce innocent persons;[50] must mean to confer expansive rights against self-incrimination and double jeopardy;[51] must mean to guarantee the right, in conditions of dignity-destroying terminal illness, to receive assistance in voluntarily bringing one's life to an end;[52] must mean to confer

---

Congressional Record, March 19, 1957, and is quoted in Peter Irons, *Brennan vs. Rehnquist: The Battle for the Constitution* (New York: Alfred A. Knopf, 1994), 34.

[47] See ibid.; William J. Brennan, Jr., "In Defense of Dissents," *Hastings Law Journal* 37 (1986): 427–38, at 435–36.

[48] Gregg v. Georgia, 428 U.S. 153, 229 (1976) (Brennan, J., dissenting).

[49] See Goldberg v. Kelly, 397 U.S. 254 (1970); see William J. Brennan, Jr., "Reason, Passion, and 'The Progress of the Law,'" *Record of the Association of the Bar of the City of New York* 42 (1988): 948–75, at 973–74; Irons, *Brennan vs. Rehnquist*, 35–36.

[50] See Paul v. Davis, 424 U.S. 693, 714 , 721–22, 734–35 (1976) (Brennan, J., dissenting).

[51] See Malloy v. Hogan, 378 U.S. 1 (1964).

[52] See Cruzan v. Director, Missouri Department of Health, 497 U.S. 261, 301 (1990) (Brennan, J., dissenting).

rights of sexual and procreational self-determination[53] and of freedom of intimate association[54] and to read whatever one wants in one's home;[55] must mean to confer the right to contest the merits and procedures of a criminal conviction over and over again.[56] These strong interpretive stances cannot well be explained by any pure-procedural standard of democratic government.

A Paradox of Pure Proceduralism

Those of us who feel strongly that Justice Brennan was on the right track might thus feel impelled to lay aside without more ado a political conception—"responsive democracy"—that its own author classifies as a pure procedural conception. We need not, however, move so hastily. We are not bound by Post's own classification of responsive democracy as a pure procedural political conception, and it might be worth pausing to consider whether that classification is or possibly could be correct.

Responsive democracy theory ties the possibility of individual self-government in politics to a society's strict adherence to the precept of absolutely unrestricted access to public discourse for every person and every view. Does the theory not, in so doing, assert certain human interests, commend certain human freedoms, and accordingly lay down foundations of political legitimacy? No doubt, the principle of unrestricted public discourse is *about* a procedural matter, a matter of governmental form. So is the principle of a fair trial about a procedural matter and a matter of governmental form. That does not mean the fair-trial principle lacks a foundation in substantive morality. (Indeed, the moral substance behind the principle shines forth in sundry issues of constitutional law, such as whether prosecutors may suppress evidence pointing toward the innocence of an accused whom they sincerely

---

[53] See Eisenstadt v. Baird, 405 U.S. 438 (1972).
[54] See Roberts v. United States Jaycees, 468 U.S. 609, 618–20 (1984).
[55] See Stanley v. Georgia, 394 U.S. 557 (1969) (Marshall, J.).
[56] See Fay v. Noia, 372 U.S. 391 (1963).

believe to be both guilty and very dangerous, or may shield juvenile complaining witnesses in child-molestation cases from having to look their alleged victimizers directly in the eye while testifying against them.)

But I want to say something stronger here than that the precept of unrestricted discourse, as it appears in responsive democracy theory, is a substantive social norm—a prescription for how to treat people (as free to speak), in view of their interests (in self-government), not just for deciding how to treat them. I want to say it is a *foundational* substantive social norm. In responsive democracy theory, uncompromising obedience to the principle of unrestricted public discourse is a prerequisite for legitimate government, a requirement that all who espouse the theory must regard as beyond all debate and all possibility of revision. It is, after all, precisely because responsive democracy theory does rest on this much of a normative foundation that Professor Post can use the theory to support the correctness of some constitutional interpretations as against others—to support, for example, interpretations that hold the line stoutly against any restriction of the content or pitch of expression in public discourse, even up to and including the case in which a magazine (it was *Hustler*) runs a drawing of a clergyman (it was Jerry Falwell) having sex with his mother in an outhouse.[57]

If responsive democracy theory does thus rest on a foundational proposition of substantive moral import, then maybe it is a closer cousin to Brennan's apparent constitutional theory than we have yet noticed. I believe it is. But that, then, returns us to the question we have already raised, about how any political conception can claim to offer a medium for anyone's, much less everyone's, self-government in politically decidable matters, when it rests the legitimacy of government on the appearance in the basic laws of the country of a specific content that inhabitants are not free to reexamine and reject. If, by the light of

---

[57] The case is Hustler Magazine v. Falwell, 485 U.S. 46 (1988). See Post, *Constitutional Domains*, chap. 4.

responsive democracy theory, Americans are not free, even by
unanimous consent, to make and enforce a law against what
Hustler did to Falwell, then how can it be said that Americans are
self-governing?

A Paradox of Constitutional Interpretation

The example we have just been using may suggest that the problem is confined to odd and extreme cases. It is not and cannot be
so confined, and we can use one of Professor Post's arguments to
illustrate why it is not.

Beyond question, the basic laws of this country include an article of assurance to all of "the freedom of speech."[58] A very large
majority of Americans doubtless approve of this article as right.
That does not mean, though, that the article is free of controversy. Controversy breaks out not over the article "itself" or in
the abstract, but over its meaning in specific applications. A recent
example is debate over the powers of public bodies and officials
to deal with virulently racist (or sexist, or sexually harassing) expression in state university environs and in other public areas and
facilities. The outbreak of this debate puts the country's virtually
unanimous commitment to "the freedom of speech" to the test
of interpretation.

Quite a few theorists these days declare themselves doubtful
of whether abstract normative expressions like "the freedom of
speech" have any ascertainable meaning as applied to worrisome
specific questions such as that of the permissibility of government
regulation of racist speech. Many of the skeptics are happy to
agree that one or another answer to the question may be *better* in
view of expected consequences for various people's lives. Their
claim is only that no answer can be said to be *truer* than another,
just as a report of what the expression "the freedom of speech"
really means. This claim runs into stormy controversy, but we

---

[58] The First Amendment provides: "Congress shall make no law . . . abridging
. . . the freedom of speech."

don't need to get embroiled in it. We can just assume that the anti-skeptics are right; there *are* such things as the true meaning of our Constitution's free-speech clause and the correct application of that true meaning to government regulations of racist speech, and that's a fact. But here is a further fact that no one denies: Facts are often unclear and subject to fair dispute, and this is surely true of facts about the applied meanings of constitutional clauses. The daily grind of American constitutional law consists of our recurrent and sometimes recalcitrant disagreements, not over whether there is a truth about the meanings of the clauses in various applications but over what those meanings are.

Parties to these disagreements—is abortion murder? does money talk?—don't usually expect to resolve them by consensus any time soon. Sometimes, though, for practical purposes, the meanings have to be publicly decided *now*. The state legislature has made a law restricting racist speech on state campuses, and the Trustees of State U. are threatening to expel Jerko and several pals for letting loose an unprovoked stream of racial epithets on a passing student of color—an admitted gross and knowing violation of the law. Can the trustees do that to Jerko? Does the First Amendment allow it? There is no escaping the question. Someone will have to decide it *now*, and decide it over sincere and reasonable disagreement. In our system, that someone would be a judge, sitting in a court of law. It could be Brennan. (I like to think he is still around.)

But then what becomes of everyone's self-government? Is there some way that everyone's self-government can possibly be preserved in or enacted by Brennan's decision in Jerko's case, about whether the basic-legal formula "the freedom of speech" covers Jerko's epithets, when the country is deeply divided over whether it does or should? Only, it would seem, on the condition that Brennan's decision, once sufficiently explained, could be seen by everyone to issue objectively and straightforwardly from some still loftier principle for government in this country that can guide and control the First Amendment's applications in contested cases. Since the Constitution and Bill of Rights are sometimes called this country's higher law, this still-loftier principle would be part of, let's call it, the country's *really* high law.

Brennan might be able to use a really-high-law principle to bring his decision in Jerko's case, about the true meaning of the First Amendment with respect to the permissibility of laws restricting racist speech, into line with everyone's self-government. It would depend on whether that really-high-law principle satisfied two conditions. First, the principle would have to be one that everyone agrees is right. Second, it would have to be one that has a more or less objective, straightforward, decisive application to the question of whether the constitutional clause in question, the First Amendment's free-speech clause, prohibits, requires, or permits the state legislature to make a law against racist speech like Jerko's. If both those conditions are met, then when Brennan uses the really-high-law principle to decide the case of Jerko, he is acting in a way that everyone can see is both legally correct and in line with their own views of what this part of the law of lawmaking ought to be. Everyone's self-government then is preserved in Brennan's decision. But if either of the conditions is not met—if there is persistent disagreement about *either* the rightness of the really-high-law principle *or* its correct application to the decision of Jerko's First Amendment claim—then Brennan deciding that claim will necessarily be fixing, on his own hook, a significant part of the content of the country's laws of lawmaking, and he will be doing so in a way with which a part of the country heartily disagrees. Under guise of "interpretation," that part of our laws of lawmaking would be written by Brennan and not, as everyone's self-government requires, by everyone. (Walt Whitman was large, or so he claimed, and contained multitudes. I happen to think that among judges Brennan was large and contained multitudes. That, however, does not make Brennan everyone, or allow it to be said that through his government I govern myself.)

What Professor Post proposes, in effect, is a certain content for the needed really-high-law principle, the use of which by Brennan to decide Jerko's First Amendment claim can bring his decision into line with everyone's self-government. That content is: assurance to all persons and all views of unprejudiced access to unrestricted public discourse in which a national identity and social order are constantly being forged. Post maintains that this principle is one to which everyone concerned about individual self-government through democracy has reason to agree. What I want to do now is see what develops if we grant Post his premise. Therefore, please assume with me that the principle of unprejudiced access for all to public discourse actually is an ultimate principle of American law for which every American, agreeing with it, can take authorship responsibility. Does it follow that, when Brennan appeals to the principle for justification of his decision about whether the Constitution's free-speech clause means to prohibit, require, or permit the making of laws restricting racist speech in public, he reduces his decision to a mere, uncreative act of application of the people's own really high law? It does not.

Ostensibly, Brennan will apply ("interpret") the really-high-law principle of unrestricted public discourse as his way of deciding the free-speech clause's meaning with regard to the legal permissibility of government regulation of racist speech. As Professor Post recognizes, though, this interpretive question is itself a strenuously and reasonably contested issue of major moral import to many Americans. Americans who answer in favor of the permissibility of regulation say that some people's indulgence in racist speech causes severe restriction of other people's ability to employ public discourse as a medium of self-government. If that contention is true, then the unrestricted-public-discourse principle can do nothing to settle the issue in Jerko's case against the permissibility of regulation, for to let it do that would be, in Post's own words, to "requir[e] that self-determination be denied to some so that it may be made available to others."[59] Moreover, as Post recognizes, the contention is not one that can be resolved by logic or reason alone. Its resolution turns partly on claims about the stigmatizing and "silencing" effects of racist speech on its targets. Those are claims about facts of personal experience.

[59] Post, *Constitutional Domains*, 320.

A person's response to them may well reflect his or her own life history, and we have in all honesty to admit that some people in this country have better firsthand knowledge than others do about both the truth and the weight of the claim. At any rate, the claim plainly is not one that can be answered by a precept of equal unrestricted access for all to government-by-public-discourse, and Brennan, therefore, cannot use any such precept as a way of getting unanimous approval of his determination of how the free speech clause applies to government regulation of racist speech in public.

It should be clear what the problem is. Americans, even if they agree on the really-high-law principle of "unrestricted access to public discourse," do not as a group have a serviceably clear fix on the content of their agreement. If we can't in all good faith agree on how to apply "unrestricted access to public discourse" to a case of such obviously major moral import (in a country with our history) as the case of racist speech, what business have we to claim agreement on any relevant principle of unrestrictedness at all? Yet the fact appears to be that we can't agree. "Unrestricted access to public discourse" turns out to be just another constitutional clause that can't be applied without someone giving it an interpretation with which many Americans sincerely and hotly disagree. What first presented itself as a question of "mere" interpretation turns out to be a morally and ideologically loaded issue about the legal limits on government that is sharply contested in our society now. The really-high-law principle of unrestricted public discourse has, it seems, turned out to be too vague and abstract to qualify as an exercise of everyone's self-government, because it leaves a major, morally loaded decision about the content of the laws of lawmaking to be made by Brennan.

We see here a paradox of constitutional interpretation, and it appears to be generalizable. Given sincere and irresolvable disagreement within society about numerous major questions of political morality, we nevertheless perceive the possibility of a consensus on laws of lawmaking, laws that do no more than establish the institutional and procedural system for further, "ordinary" lawmaking. We think it reasonable to hope that we can design a system for (further) lawmaking that everyone can honestly judge to be right or fair, and thus count themselves the authors of specific laws coming out of the system's operation, even those with which they deeply disagree. This hope rests on the idea that the laws of the lawmaking system can rest on universally appealing principles of fairness and right, ones that are abstract and general enough to rise above the concrete conflicts of interest, belief, and valuation that ordinary lawmakings cannot consensually resolve.

The theory of everyone's self-government through responsive democracy rests on exactly such a hope. Specifically, the hope is this: The principle of unrestricted public discourse being one on which all citizens can agree whatever other disagreements rage among them, all citizens can accept as "rightfully 'their own' " a system of government founded on that principle. A system founded on that principle is expected, in Post's words, to instill in citizens "a sense of participation, legitimacy, and identification."[60]

But this very abstractness of the principles of the system, on which we rely to help make the system acceptable to all, creates a problem. The matters left to be resolved by interpretation of these abstract principles are often themselves such major political-moral issues that resolutions of them one way or the other cannot readily be held separate from determinations of what the principles—in effect, the basic laws—themselves actually *are*. In such cases, the quest for self-government in politics requires that not only the initial, abstract formulations of the basic laws, but also all major interpretations of them, be accomplished in a way that responds to and satisfies everyone's interest in self-government. At the same time and inescapably, we know that effective public interpretations can only be arrived at institutionally, by nonunanimous, collective processes.

It seems there is only one way in which these institutionally dictated interpretations—Brennan's interpretations (not to say his moral readings)—can be compatible with everyone's self-gov-

[60] Ibid., 273.

ernment. Standing above the basic laws that are up for interpretation at any given time must be a still more abstract and basic set
of principles, the really high law. The principles of the really high
law must be ones that everyone can be presumed to approve,
which means they must be cast in pretty abstract terms, rising
above the issues that divide us; and yet they must at the same time
be capable of deciding objectively among contesting interpretations of the basic laws, which means they can't be *too* abstract. It
seems an impossible prescription. The really high laws, being
even more abstract than those of the constitutional clauses whose
troubled and disputed applications they are meant to control, will
even more certainly require controversial interpretations on the
way to deciding what we need for them to decide. We seem to be
caught in a sort of trap that theorists call an infinite regress.[61]

All that may be just an overwrought way of taking issue with
any proposed "non-foundational" conception of constitutional
rightness. The point is that constitutionalism—the endeavor to
place government under reason expressed as law—inevitably
means the establishment of some *a priori* fixed, non-negotiable,
non-debatable set of concretely intelligible normative first principles, I don't care whether you call them principles of the legitimacy of power or principles of the legitimacy of a debate that
determines the legitimacy of power. First principles, I mean, such
as unyielding respect for the ever-redeemable dignity of each
human being, or absolutely unrestrictedly free public discourse
come what may, come even the "silencing" (and by the scare-
quotes I don't mean to suggest that it does not really and devastatingly happen) of some people by the abusive and exploitative
communicative excesses of others.

It is now looking very much as though there cannot possibly
be, in any country, both constitutional government and self-government for everyone, except in the special circumstance of

---

[61] Compare the objections of critical legal theorists to what they call "liberal
legalism." See Frank I. Michelman, "Justification (and Justifiability) of Law in a
Contradictory World," in J. Roland Pennock and John Chapman, eds., *Justification* (Nomos XXVIII) (New York: New York University Press, 1986), 71–99, at

wholehearted acceptance by virtually all the country's people of a critical mass of substantive first principles of right government. These principles—and I don't mean by this to say they would have to be exactly the same in every country—provide the basis of "constitutional patriotism," to use the words of the German philosopher Jürgen Habermas—the "shared political culture in which citizens recognize themselves as members of their polity."[62] They are what we may call cultural commitments of constitutional democracy, ideas that in the last analysis everyone is just going to have to grow to accept, perhaps over generations, if freedom through law is going to be possible for everyone.

So back we come to the paradox of democracy, this time with added bite. Whoever cares about democracy, it appears, has to take a kind of responsibility for it, even beyond that of knowing what democracy is without waiting for democracy to tell her.[63] She has to take responsibility for becoming a national founder, basic-law-giver, and cultural prophet all rolled up in one. Or else hand that responsibility over to the judges. On this matter, Brennan's career points in the right, because the inevitable, direction.

THE REMAINING POSSIBILITY FOR SELF-GOVERNMENT IN POLITICS

Is *anyone's* self-government possible in these conditions, let alone everyone's? A while back, we left Professor Post with the worry that any procedure-independent standard of political rightness subverts self-government.[64] As I stated the point then: if there is some way in substance that the basic laws have to be in order to

---

79–81, describing the argument in Duncan Kennedy, "The Structure of Blackstone's Commentaries," *Buffalo Law Review* 28 (1979): 208–382, at 258–61.

[62] Jürgen Habermas, "Struggles for Recognition in the Democratic Constitutional State," in Charles Taylor et al., *Multiculturalism* (Princeton, N.J.: Princeton University Press, 1994), 107–48.

[63] See above, pp. 33–34.

[64] See above, pp. 39–40.

be right, then to that extent it's not rightfully up to any of us to say what the basic laws in substance shall be and thus none of us can be self-governing, at least not rightfully so. That worry, I said, was understandable. The time has now come to say it is mistaken, at least to a degree.

A minor national refounding occurs with every judicial resolution of a reasonably contested question of constitutional meaning. It is not, after all, a country's constitutional clauses as written that constitute its lawmaking system once and for all; rather, it is those clauses as from time to time interpreted and applied that constitute and reconstitute a lawmaking system in process. Perhaps that is not, in itself, a barrier to anyone's self-government. In order for you to be in a state of self-government with respect to your country's lawmaking system, it may not be necessary for you to exercise some right or power of personal control over what the system is or is becoming. Perhaps it's enough that you willingly abide by the system; and this you might do not for the reason that you control it but for the quite different and indeed contrary reason that you consider it, on reflection, to *be right*, to be in accord with what you take to be correct foundational principles for right government. That would not be a case of your being unfree in that you do not exercise a power of control over the system in force; to the contrary, it would be a case of your being free in that by your own free will, for a good reason of which you know, you approve the system in force. Abiding by the system in force over your country for the reason that you approve it as right, you would seem to be in as full a state of self-government as politics can afford.

Perhaps you'll say back to me "Fine, but that's of no help when the aim is *everyone's* self-government, because there's no chance in a modern, diverse society that everyone will agree—at least without brainwashing or equivalently horrific oppression—on the moral rightness of the same set of interpreted basic laws."[65]

---

[65] This way of looking at the problem—as one of navigating between the rock of persisting reasonable and grave disagreement and the whirlpool of oppression—is inspired by work of John Rawls. See Rawls, *Political Liberalism* (New York: Columbia University Press, 1993), 36–38.

True enough, as I have been trying to be the first to insist. But what if a person could grant her full respect to a lawmaking system—a set of interpreted basic laws—even though she does *not* consider it to be in all major respects right in its content? What if she could willingly and respectfully abide by even a seriously flawed system, because of some redeeming feature that it has aside from moral perfection or near-perfection—some feature that, she believes, gives her good and sufficient reason to respect the system? She, too, it seems, would be in a state of self-government. And what if this other, respect-garnering feature of the basic laws were one that could garner *everyone's* respect, not just hers, without oppression, in spite of substantive moral disagreement over some of the contents of these laws? In that case, the possibility of everyone's self-government would be salvaged, even on the assumption that there is no possible lawmaking system that everyone will reasonably consider to be in all major respects right in its content.

Is there any such possible redemptive feature of a set of basic laws, apart from universal agreement on the rightness of its content? If so, what is it? I would bet those questions are not irrelevant to the situations and occasional reflections of many readers of this book. (Do you feel anything like a general moral obligation to abide by the system of judicially interpreted basic laws currently in force in your country? Is that because you consider these basic laws, as currently interpreted, to be without major moral defect?)

One could take Post's "responsive democracy" theory to be saying that a person can give her respect only to those basic laws over whose interpreted content she retains some fractional direct influence through her own expressions of desire, opinion, or judgment. However, as should be clear by now, that way of motivating a person's respect for basic laws must fail for anyone believing in the existence of procedure-independent standards of basic legal rightness. If you believe there are such standards—such as that the basic laws must conform to principles of respect for the inherent dignity of the humanity in each person, or must conform to the principle of unrestricted public discourse—then the possible attribute in a set of basic laws that could possibly command your respect for them must have something to do with the chances of their being *right*. And those chances do not closely correlate with *your* having retained a shred of direct input to deciding their content, unless you believe yourself exceptionally immune to mistaken judgments about the rightness of laws.

Better for you that you don't. Because it's the fact that you don't (if you don't) on which hangs the only chance you have left to be a self-governing person, even as you abide by a lawmaking system whose constitutive laws, as interpreted, are, in all candor, not only not of your own making but not in conformity, in all major respects, with your own considered views of moral rightness.

POLITICS AND KNOWLEDGE

Here is how it might work. Your starting point would have to be that no one finally does or can know the truth about the foundational conditions of right government. And yet it couldn't be that truth in this matter is beyond reasoned argument, or just a matter of opinion or desire or power. It would have to be that truth in this matter is not *publicly ascertainable* in a company of people who, aware of human frailty and respectful of human difference, can neither (in real political time) all agree on what the truth is nor dismiss as unreasonable all positions opposed to their own. Partly, that would be because people simply differ in their deepest convictions about what is of value and worth pursuing in life. Partly, it would result from what John Rawls calls "burdens of judgment," by which he means sundry causes of disagreement about normative questions—questions about what the social rules ought to be—even among persons who, as reasonable, all observe and report honestly, argue logically, and share "a desire to honor fair terms of cooperation."[66] The causes start with the impossibility of accommodating all recognized goods in any one system of

[66] Ibid., 54–58.

institutions and the ambiguities of large moral and political concepts, and they include the difficulties of assessing complex em-
pirical evidence, of assigning relative weights to various considerations that everyone agrees are relevant, and of setting them in
comparison with each other. As Rawls says:

> To some extent (how great we cannot tell) the way we assess
> evidence and weigh moral and political values is shaped by
> our total [life] experience, . . . and our total experiences must
> always differ. Thus, in a modern society with its numerous
> offices and positions, its various divisions of labor, its many
> social groups and their ethnic variety, citizens' total experi-
> ences are disparate enough for their judgments to diverge,
> at least to some degree, on many if not most cases of any
> significant complexity.

Given the burdens of judgment, how might you think about
the rights and wrongs of basic political arrangements? You don't
have to just give up. Here are four steps that your thought might
more or less securely take:

First, you think it is of overriding moral importance that everyone who abides by ordinary laws should be able to do so not just
in order to avoid painful applications of force by the state but out
of genuine respect for the lawmaking system, constituted by a set
of interpreted basic laws, from which those ordinary laws have
issued. Why might you think that? Because you place a high value
on freedom, and it appears to you that when a person's genuine
respect for a lawmaking system gives her good reason of which
she knows to abide by whatever ordinary laws issue from that
system, including those specific ones with which she disagrees,
that person in abiding by those laws is acting freely and not under
coercion.

Second, you think there are foundational principles of moral
rightness for the basic laws and interpretations that constitute a
lawmaking system. In your mind, these would have to be principles to which everyone subject to the sway of the system has controlling reason of his or her own to agree. (The modern history
of western political thought strongly suggests that you will have

in mind principles such as toleration, freedoms of conscience and thought, respect for human dignity, equality of concern and respect for every person, free and open public discourse in a system of rule by the governed, and the rule of law.)

Third, the only ground you can see, at first, for a person's respecting a lawmaking system is that person's own considered conviction that the system's constitutive, interpreted basic laws are in all respects in accord with the foundational principles of moral rightness for such laws. But *fourth*, you see also that persistent disagreement about this very matter is inevitable, given the burdens of judgment, even among sincere and reasonable people, which means that lots of people at any time will be abiding by ordinary laws unfreely, not out of real respect for the lawmaking system but out of fear of force. Unless, that is, you can identify some basis on which everyone could freely give their respect to a set of basic-law interpretations that not everyone honestly considers to be free from serious moral error.

A fair-minded person could have a strong reason for very much wanting there to be such a thing—something that can supply a basis for the public respect-worthiness of a lawmaking system, other than its universally agreed-upon moral rightness. A fair-minded person might reflect: *I see in all reason why basic laws in the form of clauses in a constitution have to be definitely fixed, from time to time, by institutional means, and I see why major interpretations of the clauses similarly have to be definitely resolved for the country, from time to time, by institutional means. That being so, and given that there is no possibility that every institutionally authored major interpretation of every basic-law clause can match everyone's sincere and reasonable considered judgment of what is truly, morally right, it cannot be reasonable on my part to reserve my respect for only those interpretations that match my considered convictions of rightness. (Why should I thus privilege **my** own considered convictions over those of others presumably no less sincere and reasonable than I am?)*

But, your reflection continues, *I mustn't assume, either, that I am the only fair-minded person around. Countless others must be reflecting just as I am. All of us want there to be some possible feature in a lawmak-*

ing system and its constitutive basic-law interpretations that could allow us all to give it our genuine respect, so that we could all generally abide by the ordinary laws issuing out of it, even the ones we variously find to be wrong, without loss of freedom. And all of us know, too, that the feature we are looking for cannot be the entire and perfect conformity of all of the basic-law interpretations to considered convictions held by each of us regarding what is required to make such interpretations morally right. Such conformity, we all know, is not possible without oppression, given the burdens of judgment.

Reflections like those put you under pressure to find the possible feature of a set of interpreted basic laws, apart from its rightness in everyone's sight, that might make it publicly respect-worthy. Of course "apart from its rightness in everyone's sight" means apart from its substance, its content. So the alternative ground of respect-worthiness simply will have to be a procedural ground, one pertaining to the process by which current major interpretations come to have the content they do.

Perhaps now you see where I have been headed; maybe it is the *democratic character* of a country's processes of basic-law interpretation that could make the product worthy of public respect. But, if so, what could it relevantly mean for institutionally decided basic-law interpretations—*judicially* decided basic-law interpretations—to have a democratic character? And why should this democratic characteristic, whatever it is, make the difference between respect-worthy and non-respect-worthy judicial interpretations?

DISTRUST AND DEMOCRACY (RESPONSIVE DEMOCRACY WITH A DIFFERENCE)

The judiciary, we may think, has some institutional advantages over other branches of government when it comes to deciding philosophical questions.[67] Among major league baseball players, "position" players are believed to have somewhat comparable in-

---

[67] See above, pp. 22–23.

stitutional advantages—of specialization, etc.—over pitchers when it comes to batting. Yes, and most position players are lifetime .270 hitters, the best reach base less than half the time, and every palm-sweating baseball fanatic knows how success in crucial situations always rides on a wing and prayer ("a game of inches," "Please, God, let him get a hit"[68]). Everyone who has ever come to bat in major league play has been prevailingly unreliable, even Tommy Henrich.[69] That fact, obviously, is a constant, major consideration in the decisions managers often make to let pitchers bat for themselves, even in crucial situations in the late innings. A companion factor, be it noted, can be a regard for the pitcher's dignitary or prideful interest (these days, it's usually a pocketbook interest, too) in completing the game or earning the win.

So the question is, before I beat it any further into the ground: How likely is even the most capable and favorably situated judge to make serious mistakes about what democracy requires of a set of basic laws and their major interpretations? If and when our estimate of that likelihood passes beyond a certain point, the institutional advantages of the judiciary start to look like a meager excuse for not letting the people bat for themselves. (If the lifetime average of pinch-hitters were .190, how often would pitchers be lifted?)

You believe, I am now supposing, that there are procedure-independent standards of rightness for basic laws in this country now. You think these standards involve commitments both to popular political self-determination through free public discourse and to respect for individual human dignity. But you also think that discerning correct specifications and applications of these standards of right government, which really are pretty abstract and vague, is a tricky business, and you do not for a moment

[68] Yastrzemski batting in Fenway Park with two out in the bottom of the ninth and the tying run on third, October 2 (1 Tishri), 1978 (5739). He didn't, of course.

[69] Okay, I can see we maybe have a generation gap to deal with here. Tommy Henrich, a left-hand hitting New York Yankees outfielder of the thirties and forties, earned the nickname "Ol' Reliable"—from Mel Allen?—for his exceptional success when batting in the clutch. As one growing into Dodgers fanhood in the fall of 1941, let me tell you he deserved it.

believe that *anyone* judging in isolation—not yourself, not Justice Brennan—can possibly be a perfectly reliable guide to exactly what these standards require of a working, interpreted set of basic laws for this country now (regarding, for example, the "racist speech" question we considered above). It is a question, always, of the interpreter's greater or lesser reliability *and of what we can do to bolster it*. Reliability is, you think, in significant part a matter of the social and institutional conditions in which the interpreter is working. And one condition that you think contributes greatly to reliability is the constant exposure of the interpreter—the moral reader—to the full blast of the sundry opinions on the question of the rightness of one or another interpretation, freely and uninhibitedly produced by assorted members of society listening to what the others have to say out of their diverse life histories, current situations, and perceptions of interest and need.

Dignitary considerations could join these prudential (or "epistemic") ones in motivating a demand for this kind of self-exposure on the parts of the system's official interpreters of the basic laws. We would be reserving our respect for official efforts that pay *us* the respect of striving to make themselves ever more effectively available to be influenced by public debates that are fully and fairly receptive to everyone's perceptions of situation and interest and, relatedly, to everyone's opinions about justice—including, recursively, everyone's opinions about what sorts of arrangements really do make public deliberations fairly receptive to everyone's views and really do render official bodies available to the influence of those views.

For anyone thinking along such lines, two requisite attributes in any respect-worthy set of basic legal arrangements would be these: *First*, it would have to appear that a maximum feasible effort was constantly being made to get the basic laws, including all morally telling interpretations of them, *right* according to the true, procedure-independent standards of rightness that you believe there are. Quite conceivably, this maximum feasible effort could, just as Dworkin contends, include provision for a tribunal whose special business and concern it is to decide the public interpretations from time to time, or at least take the lead in deciding them. (The institutional advantages of the judiciary may not be magical, but perhaps neither are they negligible.) *Second*, this maximum feasible effort to get the basic laws and their major interpretations right would have to include arrangements for exposing the empowered basic-law interpreters to the full blast of sundry opinions and interest-articulations in society, including on a fair basis everyone's opinions and articulations of interests, including your own.

Aren't we then back to responsive democracy? Not quite, because now it is not the system's responsiveness to your input, as yours, that is giving you your reason for respecting it. What now matters to you about having your own opinions and interest-articulations registered is not some bit of leverage you exercise over what gets decided, but rather the presumptive "epistemic" or truth-finding value of your contributions to the debate, their value in helping the process toward the right answer, a value that you will not self-respectingly suppose to be less than equal to that of other people's.

Suppose you believed that the two conditions I've just sketched are actually satisfied in the current basic political arrangements and practices of your country. I am not saying that any American ought to believe it, I am merely asking you to suppose that you did. You might then find that the fact that you did allowed you to abide by the day-to-day political outcomes of these basic arrangements, out of respect for the arrangements. Would you not then freely be governing yourself, at least so far as politics are concerned?

I think that Justice Brennan may well have believed something along those lines.

BRENNAN ON DEMOCRACY

Without a doubt, Brennan believed that constitutionalism presupposes procedure-independent standards of basic-legal rightness. He believed that society's needs for equity and order require the establishment of some voting body or bodies to decide officially, for society as a whole, what those standards are and require by way of application to concrete issues and disputes. Among those bodies he would have placed national and state legislatures offering their own implicit interpretations of the Constitution, as amended, by the enactment of laws that they presumably think conform to it. But Brennan obviously believed in the strength of the institutional case for giving independent courts of law superiority over legislatures. He believed in the epistemic prudence of authorizing the Supreme Court to make constitutional law by interpreting it, in the course of passing on the constitutional validity of Acts of Congress and of the state legislatures. "Faith in democracy is one thing," he thought, but "blind faith" is another, and judicial majorities would sometimes be more reliable protectors of basic rights than popular ones.[70]

At the same time Brennan evidently also believed that political freedom—self-government—exists only when people abiding by the resolutions of basic law made by majority votes of legislatures, conventions, and courts do so out of respect for those resolutions, and that nothing can warrant the requisite respect short of the exposure of all of those who do the voting, judges included, to the full blast of what Post nicely calls democratic critical interaction.[71] In this way and to this extent, Brennan's judicial career reflects a commitment to self-government through democracy on the level of basic lawmaking. Certainly there can be no doubt that Brennan saw his Court as invested with authority and responsibility to interpret for the country a procedure-independent standard of rightness for the basics of its political regime. But I think that Brennan, enormously to his credit, saw the Court as thus empowered for only as long as it exercised its rule with a view to protecting and expanding the rights and opportunities of everyone to impress their view, democratically, upon its members and other lawmaking authorities. Accordingly, as we'll see in chapter 2, de-

[70] William J. Brennan, Jr., "The Constitution of the United States: Contemporary Ratification," *South Texas Law Review* 27 (1986): 433, 433–35; see Irons, *Brennan vs. Rehnquist*, 37.

[71] See Post, *Constitutional Domains*, chap. 4.

mocracy became, for Brennan, a name for a form of social life that values every person, and nurtures the capacity of every person as a bearer of respect-worthy political opinion, as well as for a set of constitutional arrangements designed to foster and sustain a social life of that kind.

If that be Brennanism, though, it still falls well short of the conception of everyone's self-government with which we started out. To press your views upon ruling authorities who listen is not yet to rule. To find the laws deserving of your respect is not yet to decide the laws. And what of it? Of democracy, Winston Churchill acidly remarked that it is the worst form of government except all the others that have been tried from time to time. Maybe the constitutionalist version of democracy, compromised as it is, is the worst form of democracy except all the others that have been tried from time to time. Maybe it is even the worst form of democracy except all the others that ever have been and ever will be tried. I resist that conclusion. We cannot know. What we can say is that Justice Brennan provided us with a fair test, by showing us as fine a rendition of the constitutionalist version of democracy as we and our posterity are ever likely to see.

CHAPTER 2

Brennan's Democratic Liberalism

THE JUDGE AS POLITICAL THEORIST

If a man writes frequently over many years about political matters, his collected writings would seem to make fair game for an effort to gather and restate his most general, leading thoughts on the subject of politics. But what if the man is a judge and the writings are almost exclusively his judicial opinions—in this case, William Brennan's, over a thirty-four-year span of associate justiceship on the United States Supreme Court?

There are obvious grounds for caution about attempts to pry a judge's political vision out of his judicial work product. Judges and judicial nominees regularly proclaim the irrelevance of their personally held political ideals to the work of finding and applying the country's law, and some of them doubtless believe it. Justice Brennan, though, did not believe it. He was one of our judiciary's committed moral readers of the Constitution, one of those judges for whom intellectually and morally defensible constitutional interpretation includes conscious application to the work of some more or less distinct, substantive theory of good politics.[1] Such was sometimes the justice's outspoken view while in office. "The path of formal doctrine," Brennan wrote while considering the application of the constitutional prohibition of religious establishments to the practice of opening state legislative sessions with a chaplain-led prayer, "can only imperfectly capture the nature and importance of the issues at stake in this case." Required for responsible decision would be, he said, an account of "the underlying function of the Establishment Clause," regarded as "a state-

---

[1] See above, pp. 26–28.

ment about the proper role of government in the society that we have shaped for ourselves in this land."[2]

But that Brennan was and knew himself to be a moral reader of the law does not mean he regularly wrote much in the way of express political philosophy into his opinions. In fact, he did so occasionally, but on the whole rarely. (In that respect, my sampling of his work in this chapter is not representative.) One does not ordinarily look for such stuff in such places, anyway, and not only because the men and women who get to be judges are not by and large people who have been mainly trained to write it. Justices of the United States Supreme Court are judges. Like other judges, they are in some measure captive to the need to get their work done and their convictions advanced (I mean their *legal* convictions, their convictions of the truth about constitutional law) as part of a company of peers, within the conventional constraints of judicial office. Brennan was a widely recognized master of that form of statecraft.[3] What is therefore all the more striking in his opinions is how they do, as a whole, radiate a distinct political vision through the thicket of juridical and collegial entanglements.

As a collection, Brennan's judicial works quite clearly take a well-defined political stand. Their stance is that of a political liberal on any reasonable understanding of the term. Justice Brennan was, to be sure, a *democratic* liberal—he was as dedicated to democracy as a liberal can be—and he was extraordinarily alive to the values of commitment, community, family, and faith in human life, but it is wrongheaded to label him, as some have, a collectivist, a communitarian, or an apostle of group rights.[4] If we read the Justice's judicial works as essays on politics, then liberal

---

[2] *Marsh v. Chambers*, 463 U.S. 783, 801 (1983) (Brennan, J., dissenting).

[3] For a vivid account of a dramatic case in point, see Anthony Lewis, "In Memoriam—William J. Brennan, Jr.," *Harvard Law Review* 111 (1997): 29–37.

[4] For an example of the collectivist-communitarian classification of Brennan's views, see Charles Fried, "*Metro Broadcasting, Inc. v. FCC*: Two Concepts of Equality," *Harvard Law Review* 104 (1990): 107–27, at 109, 110, 122, 125, 127.

individualism is their central teaching. Without doubt, it was a powerful impulse to that teaching that prompted Justice Brennan's expansive notions of judicial office and of constitutional-legal reason when sitting in review of governmental acts.

LIBERAL POLITICAL THOUGHT

"Liberal" is a much-abused term these days, so I had better explain right off how I am using it of Brennan. Liberalism in politics means a certain set of programmatic commitments. "[L]iberalism," as one contemporary champion puts it, "is . . . most directly a way of organizing political life that stresses the importance of freedom, individual rights, law, limited government, and public reasonableness," hence favors a constitutional language of "justice and rights" and institutional arrangements such as separation of powers and judicial review.[5] Liberals are people for whom "the language of individual rights—voluntary association, pluralism, toleration, separation, privacy, free speech, the career open to talents, and so on—is simply inescapable,"[6] as is the familiar recipe for the organization of political power:

> a publicly supported doctrine of private individual and institutional rights, a judiciary dedicated to the enforcement of those rights, a system of representation designed to mute the excesses of popular passions, a constitutional framework that impedes the hasty translation of public impulses into sweeping changes of fundamental law, and, above all, a private sphere diverse and capacious enough to mount a stern defense against public encroachment.[7]

[5] Stephen Macedo, *Liberal Virtues* (Oxford: Oxford University Press, 1990), at 4–5, 12, 207, 274–75.

[6] Michael Walzer, "The Communitarian Critique of Liberalism," *Political Theory* 18 (1990): 6–23, at 14.

[7] William A. Galston, *Liberal Purposes* (Cambridge: Cambridge University Press, 1991), 53.

On these programmatic terms, Brennan was a committed liberal in every respect, as I expect to show (in case anyone doubts) in the pages below.

Plainly, liberal constitutional ideas are inseparable from a certain outlook on human existence for which "individualism" is the apt and familiar term. Familiar as the term may be, though, the outlook it is meant to name is not always carefully described or clearly understood, and a few words now about this matter will serve us well later on. An individualist in politics is, first of all, someone whose thought about politics is constantly alert to the dimensions of singularity and severalty in human existence and experience. He is someone who sees his social world as populated by persons regardful of themselves and others as singular beings, each having a mind and life of his or her own along with some ability, at least in a congenial social environment, to take some substantial charge of his or her own mind and life—to make and pursue (within limits) his or her own judgments about what to do, what to strive for, what is good, and what is right.

Of course, the mere thought of a human *capacity* for self-direction of this kind cannot motivate any particular line of programmatic thought about politics (any more than the thought of a human capacity for counting blades of grass could do that). What's required to motivate programmatic political views is the thought of a major human *interest* in the *exercise* of the capacity. And that thought does motivate a lot—though not all—of programmatic liberal political thought, including, I think it's clear, that of William Brennan.

Notice, please, that in order to get strong programmatic motivation out of the idea of such a human interest, you do not have to take it to ridiculous extremes. You do not need the view that no life can be worth much that does not add up to a unified, coherent story from beginning to end, or even that a good life depends on the dedication of every major period within it to a unified design or plan. You don't have to think that a wonderful life cannot owe much of its shape or content to accident, or to relationships, commitments, and faiths that a person never chose but simply *has*, from birth or from circumstance. You need only the view that a person's life will be massively lacking in value if it does not acquire *enough of* its shape and direction, or its succession of shapes and directions, from aims, attitudes, commitments, and pursuits that the person willingly and consciously adopts as her own. The commitment may, as it is said, "choose me"—I am born or I am thrown into it—but it still remains to me to affirm it as mine by a conscious movement of thought.

Attributions to persons of individualized self-possession, subjectivity, and agency are certainly challengeable in theory. It is not hard in our age to stir up philosophic or psychoanalytic or social-theoretic doubts about them. The doubts do not stop liberals from making precisely such attributions, virtually automatically, at the times when they focus thought on matters of political arrangement. But notice, again, that you don't have to take the attributions to ridiculous extremes in order to get a strong programmatic motivation out of them. You don't have to think that individuals can possibly come to consciousness, acquire values and ends, or live decent lives except as socially situated beings, enmeshed in institutions, cultures, vocabularies, relationships, and groups, and dependent on them for identity and other conditions of flourishing. You can deny the reducibility of groups and organizations to individuals. You can even assert that groups and organizations sometimes flourish at the cost of the flourishing of any one or more of the individual members. Many liberal individualists take all these positions, Justice Brennan among them, as we'll see.

There is no problem about their doing so, because liberal individualism is neither a view about what gives value to the lives of individuals nor a view about the existential reality of groups. It is only the view that the lives of individuals are the ultimate moral concern for political arrangements. That does not mean that groups are not real, or that their real existence does not merit legal recognition and protection as an essential source or cause of value in individual lives.

JUSTICE BRENNAN AND LIBERAL "ROMANCE"

"Romantic" Constitutionalism and Social Emancipation

Romance takes many forms. My use of the term here draws from contemporary works by Nancy Rosenblum, Steven Shiffrin, and Roberto Unger.[8] Rosenblum presents us with Thoreau, the good neighbor minding his own business by disturbing the complacency of others:

> Minding your own business does not [for Thoreau] mean simple detachment or peaceful coexistence. One's own business requires intrusiveness, shock, and affront to others. Neighbors are irritants to one another. They impose themselves on one another's consciousness.[9]

Shiffrin's model romantic is Thoreau's neighbor Emerson, who wrote in his early essay, "The Protest," of how

> the old, halt, numb, bedrid world must ever be plagued with th[e] incessant soul [of protest]. . . . By resistance to . . . strong Custom and strong Sense—by obedience to the soul, is the world to be saved.[10]

As we see it reflected in Justice Brennan's work, the core of romantic constitutionalism lies in two, linked, commitments: to respect for individual human personality under a certain romantic conception of it, and to pursuit of a certain, emancipated state of persons-in-society. In the romantic conception of personality, the "dignity" or "infinite quality" of an individual resides in her capacity for self-revision or self-transcendence, her capacity for be-

---

[8] See Nancy L. Rosenblum, *Another Liberalism: Romanticism and the Reconstruction of Liberal Thought* (Cambridge, Mass.: Harvard University Press, 1987), 103–24, 152–86; Shiffrin, *The First Amendment, Democracy, and Romance* (Cambridge, Mass.: Harvard University Press, 1990), 140–68; Roberto Mangabeira Unger, *Passion: An Essay on Personality* (New York: Basic Books, 1984), 22–26.

[9] Rosenblum, *Another Liberalism,* 111–14.

[10] Ralph Waldo Emerson, "The Protest," in Robert E. Spiller and Wallace E. Williams, eds., *The Early Lectures of Ralph Waldo Emerson* (Cambridge, Mass.:

coming anew.[11] But that capacity is not ever exercisable by anyone in isolation from others. We all always find ourselves within the "formative contexts," as Unger calls them, of general culture, social and familial relationships, and accustomed patterns and practices of daily life—all factors that partly shape our readings of experience and understandings of ourselves. It follows that the capacity for self-revision must encompass, as Unger says, "the power of the self eternally to transcend the limited imaginative and social world that it constructs."[12] The corresponding constitutional ideal would be a set of social and political arrangements that accord great value to the capacities of individuals to transcend conventional thinking, to change and improve themselves, and to influence others and the social world.[13] And because any set of such arrangements must itself compose an important part of our formative contexts—must itself environ and condition our self-understandings—the romantic liberal commitment is to constitutional arrangements that are specially designed to make "available, in the course of ordinary politics and existence, the instruments of [their] own revision."[14]

Formative contexts, including political constitutions and governing arrangements, are always in some measure socially joint, so that to change them for one is to change them for many or for all. That is one reason why, as context-transcending agents, our freedoms as individual personalities can never be ours in isolation. The freedoms of socialized persons are interdependent; we hang

---

Harvard University Press,1972), 89–90, quoted in Shiffrin, *The First Amendment*, 146–47.

[11] Roberto Mangabeira Unger, *The Critical Legal Studies Movement* (Cambridge, Mass.: Harvard University Press, 1986), 22–23, 94.

[12] Ibid. at 92–93; Roberto Mangabeira Unger, *False Necessity* (Cambridge: Cambridge University Press, 1987), 6–7, 26.

[13] Unger, *False Necessity*, 23.

[14] Ibid. at 105. See Kenneth Casebeer, "Running on Empty: Justice Brennan's Plea, the Empty State, the City of Richmond and the Profession," *University of Miami Law Review* 43 (1989): 989–1019, at 991 (asking whether, "as human selves," we will "organize daily life around institutions that allow and demand direct ethical and political participation and responsibility, in the process [of] defining self-conscious expression").

together, or we hang separately. So the romantic liberal vision of a constituted society becomes one of institutions designed to enable individuals to choose and shape their own identities and lives, in part through vistas of possibility opened by contention over aims for the institutions that the people of a country cannot help but share. I hope you hear an echo of "responsive democracy."[15]

It is a perhaps somewhat unexpected implication of the romantic view that individuals are partly dependent for their freedom on their social formative contexts. Socially grounded expectations of behavior and culturally grounded readings of the world, and us in it, provide important parts of the field of resistance against which self-revisionary moral agency is exercisable. At the same time, it can only be from somewhere within the civilizations in which they dwell that people draw critical and evaluative resources for self-transformative exertions. The romantic-liberal ideal is itself an example. It takes its cue from "the preconceptions of [historical] liberal legal and political theory." The romantic ideal "pushes" those preconceptions to their limits:

> From the idea of a state not hostage to a faction, existing in a society freed from a rigid and determinate order of division and hierarchy, we . . . move to the conception of an institutional structure, itself self-revising, that would provide constant occasions to disrupt any fixed structure of power and coordination in social life.[16]

Right there, one can see the bridge between the romantic and the egalitarian commitments of democratic liberal constitutionalism. A chief aim of the romantic-liberal constitution must be to free "the life chances of the individual . . . from the tyranny of social categories" of "classes, sexes, and nations."[17] The benefit accrues not only to the emancipated; it is structural and systemic, and accrues to everyone. Everyone, in the romantic view, has rea-

---

[15] See above, pp. 36–38, 61.
[16] Unger, *The Critical Legal Studies Movement*, 30–31.
[17] Ibid. at 23.

son to welcome confrontation and challenge of his or her accustomed or habitual ways and values, from all quarters known and unknown. Democracy accordingly becomes not just a procedural but a substantive ideal—a commitment to empower the disempowered and reconnect the alienated. Likewise, freedom of expression figures for the romantic constitutionalist as both an individual right of self-presentation—of efficacious participation or citizenship—and a social-structural provision for imbuing social life with the enrichment, and politics with the knowledge, sparked by frictional contact with human outlooks and sensibilities other than those to which one has grown accustomed.

Justice Brennan and Personality

Now consider an arresting feature of Justice Brennan's constitutional jurisprudence (the Justice himself called it "quixotic"), his declared "immutable" opposition to capital punishment.[18] It was rooted, he said, in a basic principle of political morality inspiring the Eighth Amendment's proscription of cruel and unusual punishments: that "the state . . . must treat its citizens in a manner consistent with their intrinsic worth as human beings."[19] A punishment, Brennan wrote, must not be "so severe as to be utterly and irreversibly degrading to the very essence of human dignity."[20] Evidently, the inherent dignity of the human individual survives commission of the crime that gives rise to the punishment: "The most vile murder does not release the state from constitutional restraints on the destruction of human dignity."[21] In other words: the Constitution, morally read, commands unwavering respect for every individual's capacity for transcending biography. Where could you hope to find a clearer expression of the romantic view of personality?

[18] See William J. Brennan, Jr., "In Defense of Dissents," *Hastings Law Journal* 37 (1986): 427–38, at 432.
[19] Ibid., 432, 435–36.
[20] Ibid.
[21] Ibid.

The romantic gloss seems all the more right for Justice Brennan's notion of the essential dignity of the bearer of punishment because it fits so well with other themes we shall find coursing through the Justice's judicial work. These include his attraction to the idea of the endless contestability of just about every social-normative constraint (his own domain of constitutional law not excepted); his tolerance for rumpus and hurly-burly, for disquiet and discomfiture, again with no exemption of his own judicial province, or certainly much less than most other judges would allow; his solicitude for agitators and disturbers; his corresponding coolness toward the bureaucratic yearning for order and control; and his unique insistence on the indispensability of passion, of sympathy, to moral reason and the just exercise of power, again with no exception for legal reason or judicial power.

Exposure of Basic-Law Interpretation
to Social Contention

Justice Brennan's opinions and other writings are full of the idea that public respect for constitutional law will fail if the law is not kept responsive to the shifting controversies of social life that give concrete meaning to legal issues.[22] The idea of law's essentially fluid and contestable character made a striking appearance early in Justice Brennan's Supreme Court career, in his 1963 opinion for the Court in *NAACP v. Button*,[23] a case arising out of the state of Virginia's attempt to throw obstacles in the way of school desegregation litigation in that state. Like most states, Virginia had in force a set of rules prohibiting lawyers from recruiting plaintiffs for lawsuits that the recruits were not themselves spontaneously disposed to bring, and also prohibiting lawyers from taking

[22] See Brennan, "The Constitution of the United States: Contemporary Ratification," in Sanford Levinson and Steven Mailloux, eds., *Interpreting Law and Literature: A Hermeneutic Reader* (Evanston, Ill.: Northwestern University Press, 1988), 13–24.

[23] 371 U.S. 416 (1963).

direction from one person or organization while purporting to represent another person in court. The general idea is that society provides the litigation forum, with all its costs to society and burdens to those who get haled into court, strictly for the purpose of securing legally warranted relief from wrongdoers at the behest of those who consider themselves harmed by the wrongdoing. A lawyer, therefore, is not supposed to contrive to get a lawsuit started just because *she* thinks that something in society is broken and needs fixing, nor is she supposed to strategize and conduct a lawsuit as a vehicle for the pursuit of anyone's aims or wishes but her client's.

In the events leading up to the *Button* case, Virginia issued a somewhat unusual and complex set of rules ostensibly meant to deal with such matters, and sought to use them to prevent the NAACP from acting as instigator and coordinator of a legal campaign to desegregate the state's public schools by federal court order. Brennan's opinion for the Supreme Court barred Virginia from doing this. Many lawyers expected this result. Probably most who did expected that the Court would reach it by finding— this was still the era of "massive resistance"—that Virginia had devised or was applying the rules in question for the specific and illicit purpose of evading its own constitutional obligations, and those of its local government subdivisions, to correct its history of racial discrimination.

However, Brennan's opinion took an entirely different tack. It reasoned that constitutional litigation can sometimes be a kind of political action falling under the protection of the first amendment's guarantee of the freedoms of political speech and association. The NAACP, he wrote, may not be "a conventional political party" but

> the litigation it assists, while serving to vindicate the legal rights of members of the American Negro community, at the same time and perhaps more importantly, makes possible the distinctive contribution of a minority group to the

ideas and beliefs of our society. For such a group, association
for litigation may be the most effective form of political
association.[24]

Such reasoning has remarkable implications. It directly attacks
the notion that law stands neutrally and impartially above and
apart from politics, while tossing overboard a traditional, conservative justification of lawsuits as essentially nonaggressive and politically static actions by which people simply ask the state's assistance in securing their entitlements under preexisting, fixed, and
unquestioned rules of justice. For Brennan to treat the NAACP's
litigation-organizing activities as constitutionally protected political speech is tantamount to declaring his own courtroom a site
of a democratically legitimating public participatory process—
public discourse, we were calling it a while back—for contesting,
reconsidering, and revising the rules of justice themselves.

A similarly politicized view of the processes of litigation and
judicial decision appeared in Justice Brennan's 1986 lecture, *In
Defense of Dissents*.[25] The Justice there took issue with suggestions
that dissenting is a dangerous practice because it undermines the
myth of law's impersonal objectivity and determinacy. The legitimacy of American government, he thought, depends on the
known readiness of those who must from time to time bind the
country to contestable resolutions of constitutional meaning to
do so by moral readings. In the words of Brennan's 1987 Cardozo
Lecture, "judges must choose." What is more to the point, "the
judges who do this choosing are flesh-and-blood human beings."[26] In our language from chapter 1, they cannot credibly pose

[24] Ibid. at 431; see also William J. Brennan, Jr., "The Equality Principle: A
Foundation of American Law," *University of California at Davis Law Review* 20
(1987); 673–78, at 675–76 (associating litigation with political contention and
dissent).

[25] William J. Brennan, Jr., "In Defense of Dissents," *Hastings Law Journal* 37
(1986): 427–38.

[26] William J. Brennan, Jr., "Reason, Passion, and 'The Progress of the Law,'"
Record of the Association of the Bar of the City of New York 42 (1988): 948–75, at
953.

as sure guides to the true interpretations of the foundational principles of American government.

In Brennan's view, it is because they can't and Americans know
it that a judicial unanimity obtained by suppression of dissent cannot sustain the Court's legitimacy over the long run. Behind the
willingness of Americans to honor the rulings and acts of judicial
and other official decision-making bodies, Brennan thought there
had to be a confidence that these bodies, in return, acknowledge
everyone's right to "continue to challenge the wisdom of the result."[27] In other words, American are able to sustain a sense of
themselves as politically self-governing precisely because and insofar as official lawmakers, judges included, do not "shut down
communication as soon as a decision is reached" but encourage
indefinite debate.[28]

Brennan accordingly—and romantically—considered the
greatest dissents to be the prophetic ones, the ones that "seek to
sow the seeds for future harvest."[29] His prime example of such a
prophetic dissent was that of the first Justice Harlan, in 1896,
from the Court's endorsement of separate-but-equal in *Plessy v.
Ferguson*.[30] One hopes it was not by accident that the particular
judicial prophecy that Brennan thereby singled out for celebration, Harlan's prophecy of a "color-blind" Constitution ada-
mantly opposed to any and all race-conscious government action,
was one that in Brennan's own mature view had turned out, over
an intervening century of bitter experience, to be an honorable

[27] Brennan, *In Defense of Dissents*, 437.

[28] Ibid. Justice Brennan also quoted Chief Justice Charles Evans Hughes:
"What must ultimately sustain the court in public confidence is the character
and independence of the judges. . . . [W]hile it may be regrettable that they
cannot always agree, it is better that their independence should be maintained
and recognized than that unanimity should be obtained through its sacrifice." Id.
at 434 (quoting Charles Evans Hughes, *The Supreme Court of the United States: Its
Foundations, Methods, and Achievements* [New York: Columbia University Press,
1928]), 67–68.

[29] Ibid. at 431.

[30] 163 U.S. at 537 (1896); see Brennan, *In Defense of Dissents*, 431.

miscalculation. Brennan did not himself end his career as a champion of constitutional color-blindness. To the contrary, he ended it as a guarded defender of the use by government of minority preferences in college admissions, government contracting, and other comparable settings.[31] He stood among those who maintain that if the Constitution is to be read to command the achievement of a caste-free society,[32] then it cannot—at least it cannot yet—be read also to command color-blind lawmaking without exception. Brennan's choice of Harlan's *Plessy* dissent as his model of judicial prophecy thus neatly conveys his perception of the insuperable short-sightedness and impermanence of constitutional-legal doctrine, as harvest succeeds harvest and prophecy supplants prophecy, the old ones always proving in time to have missed their moving targets. Only "as each generation brings to bear" upon the law its "experience and understanding, its passion and reason," Brennan believed and said, is there "hope for progress in the law."[33]

Tolerance for Disorder (Even vis-à-vis Courts)

In the famous case of *Walker v. City of Birmingham*,[34] Martin Luther King, Jr., and others found themselves confronted by a flagrantly unconstitutional state-court restraining order against a planned protest march. Deciding to defy the order, they marched without first attempting an appeal to a higher court. In consequence, they were jailed for criminal contempt of court. (The silver lining was King's famous "Letter From a Birmingham Jail.")

In company with three colleagues, Justice Brennan opposed the Supreme Court's bare-majority decision to uphold this pun-

[31] See below, pp. 121–33.
[32] See *Plessy*, 163 U.S., at 559 (Harlan, J., dissenting) ("There is no caste here.").
[33] See Brennan, *Reason and Passion*, 962.
[34] 388 U.S. 307 (1967).

ishment. Chief Justice Warren[35] and Justice Douglas[36] both filed dissenting opinions, which Brennan joined. Brennan also filed a dissent of his own,[37] which the other dissenters joined. Why did Brennan, the judicial junior among the three dissenting opinion-writers in the case, feel it necessary to add words of his own? What was missing from the other dissents that he felt called upon to add?

Chief Justice Warren's dissenting opinion in *Walker* was evidently crafted to portray the case as an outlier, a virtually unique exception to a broad and strong rule that a person cannot take it upon himself to disobey a judicial order, no matter how legally erroneous, without putting himself or herself into punishable contempt of court. It was common ground among all nine Justices that a person charged with a violation of a criminal *statute* always has the right to argue its unconstitutionality as a complete defense to prosecution under it; there is never any requirement to obtain a judicial ruling of unconstitutionality prior to acting in contravention of the statute. In the minds of Warren and the majority, apparently, judicial decrees must occupy a higher plane of law-and-order sanctity than do criminal statutes and other regulatory laws, because they are society's last resort against uncontrolled disorder. All that split Warren from the majority was Warren's willingness to treat this case as the exception that proves the rule. The order prohibiting the march was *such* a "gross misuse of the judicial process," he thought, that to give it any legal standing at all would be as likely to undermine as it would be to reinforce a habit of unwavering "respect for the courts and for judicial process."[38]

Justice Brennan's separate opinion in *Walker* appears to be as much a dissent from the Chief Justice's position as from the majority's. To Brennan, both Warren and the majority were wrong in giving the social interest in judge-imposed order a virtually

[35] See ibid. at 329.
[36] See ibid. at 334.
[37] See ibid. at 338.
[38] Ibid. at 330–31 (Warren, C. J., dissenting).

automatic supremacy over that of public agitation. That, he said, is a "distortion in the hierarchy of values upon which our society has been and must be ordered," and the result is to "let loose a devastatingly destructive weapon for suppression of . . . freedoms . . . indispensable to maintenance of our free society."[39] The freedom and value that Justice Brennan thought had been subverted were, obviously, those of insurgent political action. The repressive weapon he decried was the Excalibur of the arbitrary, self-justifying judicial decree.

Brennan's *Walker* dissent evidently undertook to cut the order-keeping function of the judiciary down to size, to place it on a competitive plane of social importance with the order-keeping functions of the other branches of government and with the agitational freedoms he spoke for. In his view, the value of order preserved might sometimes have to defer to the value of order disrupted. The states' interests in maintaining unquestioning obedience to judicial orders must, Justice Brennan declared, make allowance for "collision with other and more vital interests."[40] What he apparently found intolerable in the other opinions was the "religious deference" to judicial prerogative for which he berated the majority.[41]

Solicitude for Agitators and Disrupters

Justice Brennan's high valuation of the agitational interest in *Walker* is obviously no sport. He consistently displayed an exceptional regard for agitation and eccentricity, even at some cost in public order, as a vital matter of both personal liberty and democratic social structure.[42] The 1989 flag burning case, *Texas v.*

---

[39] Ibid. at 338 (Brennan, J., dissenting).

[40] Ibid. at 344.

[41] Ibid. at 347.

[42] Of course I don't mean that such a regard was wholly peculiar to Justice Brennan. Almost every relevant opinion of his that I mention was joined by at least one other Justice (usually Marshall when it was only one). Sometimes Justice Brennan was not the author of the tell-tale opinion, but just a signatory to

Johnson,[43] is emblematic. The rhetorical hero of Justice Brennan's opinion for the Court in *Johnson*, granting first amendment protection to flag burning as an act of political protest, is not the autonomous, rebellious protester; it is the political society that protects his act of protest for sake of the self-respect of its people and of the structural value of dissent. " 'If . . . the speaker's opinion . . . gives offense,' " Justice Brennan wrote, " 'that . . . is a reason for according it constitutional protection,' "[44] because " '. . . free speech under our system of government . . . best serves its high purpose when it induces a condition of unrest, creates dissatisfaction with conditions as they are, or even stirs people to anger.' "[45] The Court's decision, he said, reaffirms

> the principles of freedom and inclusiveness that the flag best reflects . . . and the conviction that our tolerance is a sign and source of our strength. . . . [T]he image immortalized in our . . . national anthem is of the bombardment [the flag] survived at Fort McHenry. It is the Nation's resilience, not its rigidity, that Texas sees reflected in the flag . . . and it is that resilience that we reassert today.[46]

A more elaborate expression of romantic esteem for the personal spirit and social value of the agitative disturber is the Justice's celebration of political boycotts in *FTC v. Superior Court Trial Lawyers' Association*.[47] This case involved a group of private lawyers whose practices included representation of indigent defendants in the Washington, D.C., criminal courts in return for

---

it. Furthermore, in the passages that I quote from his "own" opinions, as often as not *he* is quoting (as was his wont) something previously said by a colleague or predecessor. Still, putting it all together, there is a track record here that no colleague's or predecessor's can match save possibly Thurgood Marshall's.

[43] 491 U.S. 397 (1989).

[44] Ibid. at 406 (quoting FCC v. Pacifica Foundation, 438 U.S. 726, 745 [1978] [opinion of Stevens, J.]).

[45] Ibid. (quoting Terminiello v. City of Chicago, 337 U.S. 1, 4 [1949]).

[46] Ibid. at 419.

[47] 493 U.S. 411, 436 (1990) (Brennan, J., concurring in part and dissenting in part).

compensation paid by the municipal government there. For some years leading up to the central events in the case, the government had been offering fee amounts that the lawyers, supported by bar study groups, said were too low for the level and quality of the work they did. Local officials voiced no disagreement; they just said they were broke. It was not politically possible, they said, for them either to take funds for the lawyers from elsewhere in the city budget or to increase the budget by raising local taxes.

Eventually, the association lawyers staged a highly publicized boycott of criminal defense work in Washington, stating their shared intention to take no more cases until the fees were raised. They characterized their boycott as a protest demonstration designed to mobilize political support among District voters for higher fees. Of course, the boycott also had the consequence of pressuring the government directly, by backlogging the criminal courts. The boycott in fact ended when the government agreed to increase the fees. Subsequently, the Federal Trade Commission found the lawyers to have been engaged in a price-fixing conspiracy, a violation of the antitrust laws.

The lawyers sought Supreme Court review. They claimed that the Commission's order intruded on their first amendment protected rights of political expression. In an opinion dissenting from the Court's judgment affirming the FTC's order, Justice Brennan agreed with the boycotters that their conduct had enough in it of the stuff of constitutionally favored political communication to merit first amendment protection, at least in the absence of any concrete determination (none had been made by the Commission or any court) that the boycotters actually had enough market power in the circumstances to compel concessions from their market adversary, the D.C. government. "Expressive boycotts," he wrote,

> have been a principal means of political communication since the birth of the Republic. . . . From the colonists' protest of the Stamp and Townsend Acts to the Montgomery

bus boycott and the National Organization for Women's campaign to encourage ratification of the Equal Rights Amendment, boycotts have played a central role in our Nation's political discourse. In recent years there have been boycotts of supermarkets, meat, grapes, iced tea in cans, soft drinks, lettuce, chocolate, tuna, plastic wrap, textiles, slacks, animal skins and furs, and products of Mexico, Japan, South Africa, and the Soviet Union. . . . Like soapbox oratory in the streets and parks, political boycotts are a traditional means of "communicating thoughts between citizens" and "discussing public questions."

. . . .

By sacrificing income that they actually desired, and thus inflicting hardship on themselves as well as on the city, the lawyers demonstrated the intensity of their feelings and the depth of their commitment. The passive nonviolence of King and Gandhi are proof that the resolute acceptance of pain may communicate dedication and righteousness more eloquently than mere words ever could. A boycott, like a hunger strike, conveys an emotional message that is absent in a letter-to-the-editor, a conversation with the mayor, or even a protest march. . . . In this respect, an expressive boycott is a special form of political communication. . . .

Another reason why expressive boycotts are irreplaceable as a means of communication is that they are essential to the "poorly financed causes of little people." . . . It is no accident that boycotts have been used by the American colonists to throw off the British yoke and by the oppressed to assert their civil rights. . . . Such groups cannot use established organizational techniques to advance their political interests, and boycotts are often the only effective route available to them.[48]

[48] Ibid. at 447–48, 450–51.

More tortuous, but in the end similarly disposed, are Justice Brennan's opinions dealing with regulation by public school administrators of students' expression while in school. The topic is thorny, as Justice Brennan explained, because of the "weighty and delicate" combination of socialization tasks we impose on public educators. The Justice said that educators are supposed to inculcate (in part by their own example of respect for "democratic liberties") an appreciation of " 'fundamental values necessary to the maintenance of a democratic political system . . . ;' " to "convey to our young the information and tools required . . . to survive in [and] contribute to civilized society"; and to "nurture students' social and moral development by transmitting to them an official dogma of 'community values.' "[49]

Over two cases, two years apart, we find a shift in Justice Brennan's thought about how the conflicts among these objectives are to be sorted out constitutionally. In the *Fraser* case of 1986, he concurred in a judgment upholding school discipline for a high school student's lewdly suggestive speech in a school assembly.[50] He so voted, the Justice explained at the time, "in light of the discretion school officials have to teach high school students how to conduct civil and effective public discourse, and to prevent disruption of educational activities."[51] That formulation comes down hard on offensiveness and incivility. It lumps breaches of decorum together with disruptions of educational activities.

By the time of the *Kuhlmeier* case in 1988, however, Justice Brennan had changed his tune. Protesting against a school's censorship of school newspaper stories on "sensitive" matters of family break-up and teenage sex, the Justice now drew the line firmly *between* incivility and disruption. The speech of students at school, according to the Justice's latest word on the subject, is

[49] Hazelwood School Dist. v Kuhlmeier, 484 U.S. 260, 277–78 (1988) (quoting Ambach v. Norwick, 441 U.S. 68, 77 [1979], and Board of Educ. v. Pico, 457 U.S. 583, 564 [1982] [Brennan J.] [plurality opinion]).

[50] Bethel School Dist. v. Fraser, 478 U.S. 675, 687 (1986) (Brennan, J., concurring in the judgment).

[51] Ibid. at 687 (Brennan, J., concurring in the judgment).

censorable only on the ground that it materially impedes specific educational activity, threatens actual disorder, or violates legal rights.[52] Fraser's "lewd endorsement of a student-government candidate," Justice Brennan retrospectively and somewhat lamely intimated in his *Kuhlmeier* opinion, was censorable only because it "might so extremely distract an impressionable high school audience as to interfere with the orderly operation of the school."[53] But speech at school the Justice now found not censorable on the ground that its content or style conveys a morality inimical to the school's, or risks wounding sensibilities,[54] or even (here the Justice was quoting and it seems gently mocking the majority's opinion) violates " 'the shared values of a civilized social order.' "[55] To censor on those grounds, the Justice now contended, would display a "contempt for individual rights" that is "particularly insidious from [those] to whom the public entrusts the task of inculcating in its youth an appreciation for the cherished democratic liberties that our Constitution guarantees."[56]

Disparagement of Bureaucratic Interests

Justice Brennan's protectiveness toward agitators and disturbers merges with another feature of his romantic-liberal side that I have mentioned, his relative dismissiveness of managerial interests in order, calculation, and control. He worked vigorously to expand legal protection for those whom he saw embattled by officialdom's ambitions, automations, fixations, and routines. He was an architect[57] and advocate[58] of federalized safeguards for

[52] See *Kuhlmeier*, 484 U.S. at 279, 289–90 (Brennan, J., dissenting).
[53] Ibid. at 279.
[54] See ibid. at 577.
[55] Ibid. at 286.
[56] Ibid. at 290.
[57] Malloy v. Hogan, 378 U.S. 1 (1964). My citations of course do not even begin to document Brennan's exercise of activist influence by his encouragement and support of decisions written by colleagues.
[58] See William J. Brennan, Jr., "State Constitutions and the Protection of Individual Rights," *Harvard Law Review* 90 (1977): 489–504, at 492–93.

individuals confronting state police and prosecutors; a contender for aggressive relief against the vestiges and remainders of Jim Crow;[59] a defender of children's rights against official callousness,[60] overbearingness,[61] and tutelary subjection;[62] and in general a champion of effective legal remedies against governmental lawlessness.[63]

The other side of this coin is Brennan's campaign, only partially successful, to make governmental bodies and officials easily and directly suable by citizens seeking compensation for harms done to them in violation of constitutional rights. In a dizzying succession of technical legal contexts—determining the scopes of eleventh amendment[64] and statutory immunities;[65] determining which levels and types of governments are and are not "persons" rendered liable to suit by federal civil rights laws;[66] determining when constitutional law makes state officials accountable for traditional legal wrongs such as defamation and destruction of property;[67] determining whether provisions of the bill of rights (not

[59] See Green v. County School Bd., 391 U.S. 430 (1968); Keyes v. School Dist. No. 1, 413 U.S. 189 (1973).

[60] See DeShaney v. Dept. of Social Services, 489 U.S. 189 (1989) (Brennan, J., dissenting from the Court's refusal to recognize any affirmative governmental duty to protect defenseless infants against physical abuse by parents).

[61] See New Jersey v. T.L.O, 469 U.S. 325, 353 (1985) (Brennan, J., dissenting in part from the Court's relaxation of constitutional protections against official searches of personal effects—the purse of a student caught smoking a cigarette— when the searcher is a school teacher or administrator and the searchee is a student).

[62] See *Kuhlmeier*, n. 52, above.

[63] See Goldberg v. Kelly, 397 U.S. 254, 261 (1970) (holding that a statutory entitlement to welfare benefits is property constitutionally protected against peremptory or arbitrary administrative deprivation).

[64] See Edelman v. Jordan, 415 U.S. 651, 687 (1974) (Brennan, J., dissenting).

[65] See Owen v. City of Independence, 445 U.S. 662 (1980) (holding that municipalities enjoy no implied immunity from suit under the basic federal civil rights law, 41 U.S.C. §. 1983).

[66] See Monell v. Dept. of Social Services, 436 U.S. 658, 690 (1978) (holding that municipalities, unlike states, are "persons" subject to liability for civil rights violations under federal statutes).

[67] See, e.g., Paul v. Davis, 424 U.S. 693, 714 (1976) (Brennan, J., dissenting from a holding that a state officer's false, public denunciation of plaintiff as a

only the fourth amendment's guarantee against unwarranted searches and seizures but also the fifth amendment's guarantee against uncompensated taking of property) directly mandate the liability of violators to monetary recoveries[68]—Justice Brennan stood opposed to letting governments and their officials fend off liability to pay compensation to those whom their actions wrongfully harm. Plainly, he was the least susceptible of Justices to pleas that exposure to such a liability impairs governmental efficiency, deters governmental application, or, by rendering life in office financially hazardous, hinders the government's ability to attract the best talent to public service.

To Justice Brennan, evidently, officialdom's needs for a special immunization against hazards of legal exposure that the rest of us manage to put up with simply didn't seem symmetrical with those of individual citizens for vindication of their rights. (He would have agreed to letting Paula Jones's case proceed against Clinton while President.) His view that a sufficiently determined government has power enough to see to its own needs without special judicial favors at the expense of ordinary citizens came through clearly in the *Trial Lawyers* case. To complaints that the lawyers' boycott was an attempt to coerce the District government into complying with their salary demands by creating a crisis in the D.C. criminal courts, Brennan responded that the government had the power, *in exremis*, to compel provision of the services by writing a law requiring their provision by the local bar, *pro bono*.[69]

---

known shoplifter is not civilly actionable as a deprivation of liberty without due process of law contravening the Fourteenth Amendment and civil rights statutes).

[68] See San Diego Gas Co. v. San Diego, 450 U.S. 621, 636 (1981) (Brennan, J., dissenting from the Court's refusal to reach the merits of a claim for monetary compensation for loss inflicted by a regulation eventually held to be an unconstitutional taking of property, and upholding the claim); Bivens v. Six Unknown Named Agents, 403 U.S. 388, 397 (1971) (holding that the fourth amendment's proscription of unreasonable searches implies a civil-damages remedy against miscreant officers, obtainable in the federal courts, despite the absence of congressional provision by legislation for such a remedy).

[69] *Trial Lawyers*, 493 U.S. at 451–52.

Agitation and management are natural adversaries, as Justice Brennan's judicial work repeatedly reminds us. In the 1963 case of *Columbia Broadcasting System v. Democratic National Committee*,[70] Brennan refused to join the Court in granting greater first amendment weight to the editorial discretion of broadcast companies than to uncensored access to the airwaves by political advertisers willing to pay the usual freight. Striking the balance the Court's way, said the Justice, "seriously overestimates the ability—or willingness—of [profit-motivated] broadcasters [responding to mainstream demand] to expose the public to the 'widest possible dissemination of information from diverse and antagonistic sources.' "[71] In 1966, we find Brennan joining Justice Douglas's dissent from a decision sustaining the right of a state as owner of real estate to remove from a jailhouse driveway a crowd of civil-rights protesters who hadn't interfered with the jail's vital functions but had "blocked" the driveways—although, according to the dissent, it wasn't clear that they wouldn't have moved out of the way upon request.[72] In 1976, he dissented, with only Justice Marshall for company, from a decision upholding the right of the U.S. Army, as proprietor of Fort Dix, to forbid, totally and absolutely, any and all political speeches and events within the Fort. In Brennan's stated view, the correct constitutional test looks not to the prerogatives of land ownership but to whether the speech activities will be basically incompatible with the activities to which the locale is primarily dedicated by its governmental owner.[73] He followed up with a 1981 dissent from a decision upholding the Minnesota State Fair's ban on distribution of literature anywhere on the fair grounds except from an authorized booth obtainable only on payment of a substantial rental. He found the ban a constitutionally objectionable restriction on the

---

[70] 412 U.S. 94 (1973).

[71] See ibid. at 187 (Brennan, J., dissenting) (quoting Associated Press v. United States, 326 U.S. 1, 20 [1945]).

[72] See Adderley v. Florida, 385 U.S. 39, 48, 51–52 (Douglas, J., dissenting).

[73] See Greer v. Spock, 424 U.S. 828, 860–61 (1976) (Brennan, J., dissenting).

exercise of free-expression rights, improperly based on a "general, speculative fear of disorder."[74]

Connick v. Myers (1983)[75] is an especially revealing case. At issue was the claimed first amendment right of Myers, a disaffected lawyer in a state District Attorney's office, to circulate among fellow staffers a questionnaire soliciting their views about work-assignment policies, office morale, the need for a grievance committee, confidence in their supervisors, and the existence of management pressure to engage in extra-curricular partisan political work. Writing for four dissenters, Brennan tussled with the majority over the degree of "public concern" attached to the issues to which Myers' questionnaire was directed. He said that judicial deference to the employer's judgment is out of order "when public employees voice critical views concerning the operations of the agency for which they work."[76] But beyond thus emphasizing the weight of the public's interest in hearing from Myers, Brennan also made light of the opposing interest, criticizing both the government employer and the Court majority for overreacting to speculative fears of workplace disruption, and for giving in to thin-skinned anxieties about the "discomfort and unpleasantness' " of receiving vocal criticism.[77] Brennan drew from a Vietnam era case protecting symbolic protest (black armbands) by students while attending school the lesson that nothing could justify suppression short of " 'material[] and substantial[] interference with the requirements of appropriate discipline in the operation' " of the workplace.[78]

[74] See Heffron v. International Society for Krishna Consciousness, 452 U.S. 640, 662 (Brennan, J., concurring in part and dissenting in part).

[75] 461 U.S. 138, 156 (1983).

[76] Ibid. at 163–66, 168.

[77] Ibid. at 169 (quoting Tinker v. Des Moines School Dist., 393 U.S. 503, 509 [1969]).

[78] Id. (quoting *Tinker*). The references to the *Tinker* case lead me to disagree with Steven Shiffrin's complaint that Justice Brennan's opinion in *Connick* overlooked the values of dissent and nonconformism "at stake" in that case. See Shiffrin, *The First Amendment*, 77.

In *Brown v. Glines*,[79] Justice Brennan dissented alone from the Court's grant of constitutionality to Air Force requirements of preclearance by base commanders of any written material to be posted or circulated on a base.[80] He argued that the "expertise" claimed by military commanders is likely to be "tainted" by "the natural self-interest that inevitably influences their exercise of the power to control expression," and that vaguely defined interests in "discipline or military efficiency" tend to merge into "officials' personal or bureaucratic preferences."[81] In *Goldman v. Weinberger*,[82] Justice Brennan dissented on similar grounds from the Court's decision allowing the Air Force to prohibit a Jewish officer from wearing his yarmulke while on duty (as a doctor) in the overriding interest of esprit de corps sustained by uniformity of dress.[83]

Justice Brennan's opinions in some of these cases show nicely the linkage between a romantic regard for personality and an emancipatory aim for society.[84] In *Glines*, the Justice observed that what a commander perceives as a "threat to discipline and morale will often correlate with the commanding officer's personal and political biases."[85] In *Goldman*, reminding us that "definitions of necessity are influenced by . . . experiences and values," he warned that "the military, with its strong ethic of conformity and unquestioning obedience, may be particularly impervious to minority needs and values." A "critical" function of the religion clauses, he said, is to protect minority religions from disparagement of practices that the mainstream finds "unimportant, because unfamiliar."[86] Most striking is Justice Brennan's opinion in the *Pacifica*

[79] 444 U.S. 348 (1980).
[80] Ibid. at 361 (Brennan, J., dissenting). The serviceman in this case wanted to circulate petitions regarding Air Force standards for personal grooming, for forwarding to federal government officials.
[81] See ibid. at 370.
[82] 475 U.S. 503 (1986).
[83] See ibid. at 513 (Brennan, J., dissenting).
[84] See above, pp. 70–71.
[85] See *Glines*, 444 U.S. at 365 (Brennan, J., dissenting).
[86] *Goldman* at 518, 524.

case,[87] dissenting from the Court's endorsement of the FCC's claim of authority to punish a broadcaster for wafting George Carlin's seven filthy words toward unsuspecting people's radio sets. The Court, wrote the Justice in an opinion joined by Justice Marshall, evinces

> a depressing inability to appreciate that in our land of cultural pluralism, there are many who think, act, and talk differently from the Members of this Court, . . . who do not share their fragile sensibilities, and who, for a variety of reasons, including a conscious decision to flout majoritarian conventions, express themselves using words that may be regarded as offensive by those from different socio-economic backgrounds. In this context, the Court's decision may be seen for what . . . it really is: another of the dominant culture's inevitable efforts to force those groups who do not share its mores to conform to its way of thinking, acting, and speaking.[88]

In *Goldman*, Justice Brennan treated "minority needs and values" as an object of concern and regard. In *Pacifica*, he drew attention to differences and conflicts among "cultures" and "groups." Was he, in these cases, thinking as a collectivist or communitarian? Was he thinking in terms of group rights? Let us see.

COMMUNITY

What Is "Communitarian" in American Constitutional Debate?

A communitarian, I take it, is someone for whom it sometimes makes sense to think of human groups, organized or unorganized—families, enterprises, religious faiths, social movements, ethnic communities, clubs, towns, nations, classes—as having

---

[87] FCC v. Pacifica Foundation, 438 U.S. 726, 762 (1978).
[88] Ibid. at 513 (Brennan, J., dissenting).

"group" interests, meaning interests that the group as a unit is conceived to have, above and beyond any interests that individuals may have in the fate or the proceedings of the group. Communitarians, I further take it, are committed to the proposition that it is sometimes right to give decisive normative weight to a group interest even at considerable cost to what would otherwise appear to be reasonable claims and concerns of individuals. Similarly, I take it, to advocate "group rights" is to take the position that the moral weight of a group interest can give the group an entitlement to some form of governmental action or forbearance; that this entitlement can often prevail over competing public considerations; and that among the public considerations that may have to give way are conceptions of what sort of treatment is normally due to individuals taken one by one. (That is how, for example, advocacy of affirmative action may be construed as a form of recognition of group rights.)

The foregoing are "strong" definitions of communitarianism and group rights. By that, I mean they are designed to exclude cases that more casual uses of these terms would include. Here is an example of what I mean by a more casual use. Many people today take the view that the survival of American Indian nations and their cultures is a matter of such great moral weight that the nations have morally justified claims against the state for aid and protection. Suppose you ask an advocate of this view her reasons for it and she responds: "Because [meaning *only* because] of the difference that national survival makes for the lives that many Indian people are thereby enabled to lead." Is her view then a communitarian one? Is she advocating group rights? Not in the strong senses of those terms that I am stipulating here. She is not speaking in any essential or indispensable way of an interest of the nation, not saying or advocating anything that can't be said or advocated—even if a bit more clumsily and coldly—in terms of certain interests, and their moral weight, that she believes individuals to have in the fate of the nation.

My definitions thus exclude a good deal of what often passes for communitarian or group-rights talk in American political discourse. I have cast them that way intentionally, with a view to attacking some confusions about both American political liberalism and Justice Brennan's outlook. In response to communitarian critics and with the aid of Brennan's example, I want to convey that American political liberalism is a philosophy both decidedly individualist and yet decidedly non-"atomist." In response to libertarian critics and with the aid of Brennan's example, I want to convey that democratic liberalism is a coherent and attractive political position, free of anything anyone need remotely see as an ominously totalitarian trafficking with group rights. In sum, I want to convey that there can be a broadly appealing, community-conscious (but not communitarian), wholly authentic brand of democratic-liberal individualism, and that Brennan represented it.

Communitarianism, True and False

Let us, then, begin with this question: Are there *any* strong-sense communitarians influentially participating in American constitutional discourse?

We may sometimes hear, or think we do, people speaking in dead earnest of groups as if they are singular live subjects. People may speak, for example, of group consciousness, group agency, or group well-being. The strongest idea of group consciousness would be that groups, social wholes, are the real sites of experiential states and processes—affect and desire, sensation and perception, reflection and judgment, imagination and will. The strong idea of group agency is different, but only a little less staggering to ordinary intuitions. It is not that no one, really, separately experiences anything, but that no one, really, separately *does* anything. The idea is that however loud and clear may be your or my impression that we calculate, plan, decide, and act as individuals, these impressions of ours are illusory; all that really act (insofar as anything at all can be said to act) are social systems responding to systemic needs and environmental disturbances. Think, in the extreme, of ant colonies.

It seems safe to say that such strong ideas of group consciousness and agency have little if any purchase in American constitutional culture. Most if not all participants in the culture could
hardly help but find them mysterious. At best, some of us might
charitably recast them as metaphors for social conditions of
human existence that few would seriously deny—the dependency
of each person's ability to act effectively on the acts of others, and
the deep insinuations of cultures, ideologies, languages, relationships, and various group identifications and attachments into all
of the perceptual, interpretative, voluntary, and sympathetic processes that occupy and largely compose the consciousness and
self-consciousness of any individual.

But now comes a complication. Those of us (is it all of us?) who
incorrigibly proceed in life on the basis of the apparent, exclusive
reality of individual consciousness and agency may still sometimes, for some purposes, take the correct aim for social arrangements to be the well-being of some group or of society as a whole.
Certainly, the sense that experience and agency accrue only to
individuals does not logically stop anyone from believing that the
fate of the group—its aggregate wealth or power, its world-his-
torical glory, the godliness of its culture, whatever—can trump
any and all concerns about individuals in some larger scheme of
importance or value. Now, this is more than a logical possibility;
it is a position sometimes taken by influential participants in
American constitutional debates.

Chief Justices are by definition influential, so consider an example from Chief Justice Rehnquist's opinion for the Supreme
Court in the 1990 *Cruzan* case.[89] That was a case of a totally and
irreversibly comatose young auto accident victim, one to whom
doctors gave an absolute zero chance of recovery from her "persistent vegetative" state, whose parents sought to have her removed from mechanical life support. Missouri's rule of law for
cases of this kind did not totally prohibit doctors from complying
with such requests in all circumstances, but it did make it a crime

[89] Cruzan v. Director, Dep't of Health, 497 U.S. 261 (1990).

to do so without clear evidence of the patient's prior specific expression of a considered desire not to be kept alive, in such circumstances, by artificial means.

A rule of that sort might conceivably be justified by the state's acceptance of a responsibility to make sure that a person's life is never terminated against her will or her interest, by decision of someone who is both not that person and not strictly looking out for that person's interest. Such a justification, rooted in an ultimate concern for individuals, would not be a communitarian one under our strong definition. However, it was not entirely on such a basis that our Chief Justice explained his decision. According to him, a state may assert, in addition, an interest of its own (or of society's) that *overrides* individuals' interests. A state, he wrote, "may properly decline to make judgments about the 'quality' of a life that a particular individual may enjoy and simply assert an unqualified interest in the preservation of human life *to be weighed against the interest of the individual.*"[90]

Now, let us proceed here with care. There seem to be two quite different ways of understanding what Rehnquist had in mind. His words unquestionably suggest that a state may appropriately act to preserve an ethical climate in which the continuation of human life is strongly valued regardless either of "quality" or of the desire of anyone in particular for its continuation in his or her person. (In a case decided well after Brennan's retirement, Rehnquist called the state's interest partly "symbolic and aspirational.")[91] But a state may have two quite different sorts of reasons for such a goal. Rehnquist may have meant—I think his language points to this—that a state may appropriately act in defense of that sort of ethical climate just for its own sake, because it is right or good or virtuous, or simply pleasing to a majority, utterly without regard to any interests individuals may take in their own lives. But possibly he meant only that a state could reasonably judge that its support and inculcation of the idea of the sacredness of human life

---

[90] Ibid., 281 (emphasis supplied).
[91] Washington v. Glucksberg, 117 Sup. Ct. 2258, 2302 (1996).

is one good way to protect the interests of individuals against wrongful and harmful abuse and neglect. (Incest taboos are sometimes similarly explained.) If Rehnquist's meaning was the former, he was voicing a strong communitarian idea. If the latter, he was conceiving of the state's ethical-climatic interest in what we may call a false-communitarian way—as strictly a means, without value in itself, to the end of protecting interests of individuals.

Either way, sharp retorts came forth from Justices Brennan and John Stevens. "The State," Brennan wrote, "has no legitimate interest in someone's life, completely abstracted from the interest of the person living that life, that could outweigh the person's choice to avoid medical treatment."[92] That language is a flat rejection of any strong communitarian message that the Chief Justice might have intended, for it clearly would disallow the state from coercing anyone to live on for the sake of a majority's concern about ethical climate as such. But Brennan also went on to take issue with whatever false-communitarian argument Rehnquist might have been offering. As Brennan saw the case, it involved a contest between the state and Nancy Cruzan's parents over the parents' wish to exercise a life-and-death choice on Nancy's behalf. A state has a legitimate interest in safeguarding a helpless person's choice, Brennan said, but it may not pursue that interest by simply "appropriating" that choice when close relatives of unimpeached motivation are standing by ready to make it. What the state must rather do in such a case, Brennan seemed to say, is back off because that is what a sensitive regard for *the patient* requires:

> Family members are best qualified to make substituted judgments for incompetent patients not only because of their

---

[92] Ibid. at 313 (Brennan, J., dissenting). See also id. at 357 (Stevens, J., dissenting): "Lives do not exist in abstraction from persons . . . [and] to pretend otherwise is to deny the personhood of those whose lives are defined by the State's interests rather than their own." Compare Robin West, "Narrative, Responsibility and Death," *Maryland Journal of Contemporary Legal Issues* 1 (1990): 161–77, 173 ("[T]he conservatives on the Court have responded to a very real need to honor and value life, but by . . . trivializing rights, they have refused to honor that which renders life of value.").

peculiar grasp of the patient's approach to life, but also because of their special bonds with him or her . . . . It is they
who treat the patient as a person, rather than a symbol of
a cause.

[A] State may exclude from consideration anyone having im-
proper motives. But a State generally must either repose the
choice with the person whom the patient himself would most
likely have chosen as proxy or leave the decision to the patient's family.[93]

The difference, then, between the conservative, false-communitarian Rehnquist and the liberal, individualist Brennan lay in their
opposite responses to the state's claim of sovereign responsibility
and prerogative to define and protect the interests of individuals,
at least those who cannot act for themselves. Brennan on this
occasion took what may look like an anti-statist position, but
which we do better to regard as a pro-individualist position. (The
two are not the same, as we'll see.) His record as a whole clearly
demonstrates both flat rejection of strong communitarianism
and a systematic preference for individual self-responsibility and
self-direction over state parentalism. Any lingering impressions
to the contrary can perhaps be blamed, at least in part, on some
tricky facts of American constitutional-legal rhetoric, to which
we now turn.

Rhetoric and Vision

"State interests" and liberal social structure. The fact is that American constitutional disputants, without exception, do regularly in-
voke in their arguments such facially collectivistic notions as
those of "state" or "governmental" interests. They can hardly
help doing so, because, in American constitutional-legal discourse (as in constitutional-legal discourse around the world),

[93] *Cruzan* at 327–38 (Brennan, J., dissenting) (quoting *In Re Jobes*, 529 A.2d
434, 445 [N.J. 1987]).

the rights protected by the bill of rights are always presumptive (some of them extremely strongly so), never absolute. All constitutional rights are subject to override by a sufficiently weighty interest attributed to some government or state. Of course, that is not necessarily a sign of the universal communitarianism or collectivism of constitutional-legal discourse. It may only be a sign that individuals' rights and interests can come into conflict, or that it may sometimes make good liberal-individualist sense to limit or qualify rights for the sake of what we may term a liberal-individualist social structure or climate. Suppose you think the Constitution is dedicated to the "substantive liberal values of [individual] freedom, equality, and human dignity."[94] Suppose you also think that government may sometimes have occasion to act effectively toward the achievement of these values in social life as we really live it—even, sometimes, through measures that deviate from the sort of regard for individuals that liberal principles normally demand. How are you going to express yourself if deprived of the rhetoric of legitimate state interests?

In short, the ostensible collectivism or communitarianism of "state interest" talk may be superficial, because the judicially consecrated state interests may turn out to be either liberal-individualist rights—as when the Court justifies a clear restriction of political expression by its aim of protecting "residential privacy,"[95] or justifies a clear restriction on freedom of association by its aim of "eradicating discrimination against its female citizens"[96]—or liberal social-structural concerns—as when the Court justifies a

[94] Stephen A. Gardbaum, "Why the Liberal State Can Promote Moral Ideas After All," *Harvard Law Review* 104 (1991): 1350–71, at 1352 (1991); see Joseph Raz, *The Morality of Freedom* (Oxford: Oxford University Press, 1986), 162, 425–29.

[95] Frisby v. Schultz, 487 U.S. 474, 488 (1988) (O'Connor J.) (upholding a municipal ordinance that prohibited the picketing of any residence).

[96] See Roberts v. United States Jaycees, 468 U.S. 609, 623 (1984) (Brennan, J.).

minority racial preference in the distribution of broadcast licenses by its aim of increasing "broadcast diversity."[97]

Some constitutional norms refer directly to joint or shared conditions of institutional or social structure, with no intermediating or explanatory reference to the severable rights or interests of any individual. For example, when the Supreme Court grants constitutional protection to political speech funded by corporations, the Court does not pretend that a corporation is a person entitled to liberty. (Not yet, anyway.)[98] Nor does the Court equate a restriction on corporation-funded speech with a denial of personal freedom of expression to the corporation's individual owners. Rather, the Court says that all speech addressed to matters of political moment is "expression that the First Amendment was meant to protect" as "indispensable to decisionmaking in a democracy."[99]

Even when an individual's liberty is directly in question, structural and systemic values often enter into constitutional-normative argument. Recall Justice Brennan's opinion for the Court in *Texas v. Johnson*. The Justice responded similarly to a plea that dismissing government workers for reasons of partisan patronage is constitutionally permissible because patronage serves effective democracy by sustaining party organization and loyalty:

> [A]t bottom we are required to engage in the resolution of conflicting interests under the First Amendment. . . . The illuminating source for which we turn in performing the task is the system of government the First Amendment was intended to protect, a democratic system whose proper functioning is indispensably dependent on the unfettered judgment of each citizen on matters of political concern. . . . [P]olitical parties [can be] nurtured by other, less intrusive

---

[97] See Metro Broadcasting, Inc. v. FCC, discussed at length below.

[98] But see Austin v. Michigan Chamber of Commerce, 494 U.S. 652, 699 (1990) (Kennedy, J., dissenting) ("[T]he Act discriminates on the basis of the speaker's identity. Under the Michigan law, any person or group other than a corporation may engage in political debate over candidate elections . . . .").

[99] First Nat. Bank of Boston v. Bellotti, 453 U.S. 765, 776–77 (1978).

... methods. ... [A]ny contribution of patronage dismissals to the democratic process does not suffice to override their severe encroachment on First Amendment freedoms.[100]

Social-structural conditions such as openness to public controversy are purely collective goods. Promoting such goods by coercion of law is an ostensibly collectivist project. (Judicial review is a form of legal coercion. The coercion of law was, for example, implicitly mobilized against the state of Texas by the Supreme Court's action in *Texas v. Johnson*.) But insofar as the aim is to maintain a structure conducive to basically individualistic, democratic-liberal ideals according to some reasonable conception of them, the collectivism is skin-deep.

Justice Brennan adduced democratic-liberal structural concerns in asserting and explaining the Constitution's protection of false defamatory[101] or otherwise invasive[102] speech; its protection of press access to criminal trials;[103] and its prohibition against establishments of religion: "If the Court had struck down legislative prayer today," he wrote in one of his more memorable opinions, "it would likely have stimulated a furious reaction. But it would also, I am convinced, have invigorated both 'the spirit of religion' and 'the spirit of freedom.' "[104] The Constitution protects freedom of intimate association, Brennan explained, because intimate associations play "a critical role in the culture and traditions of the Nation by cultivating and transmitting shared ideals and beliefs; they thereby foster diversity and act as critical buffers between the individual and the power of the State."[105] Obviously,

---

[100] Elrod v. Burns, 427 U.S. 347, 371–73 (1976). In many other cases, of course, Justice Brennan found occasion to stress the individual-libertarian side of freedom of expression. See, e.g., Columbia Broadcasting System v. Democratic National Committee, 412 U.S. 94, 192–93, 201 (1973) (Brennan, J., dissenting).

[101] See, e.g., New York Times Co. v. Sullivan, 376 U.S. 254 (1964).

[102] See, e.g., Time, Inc. v. Hill, 385 U.S. 374 (1967).

[103] See Richmond Newspapers, Inc. v. Virginia, 448 U.S. 555 (1980) (Brennan, J., concurring in the judgment).

[104] Marsh v. Chambers, 463 U.S. 783, 822 (1983) (Brennan, J., dissenting).

[105] Roberts v. United States Jaycees, 468 U.S. 609, 618–19 (1984).

this sort of appeal to social-structural motivations for constitutional protection of individual rights[106] cannot be the mark of a collectivist or communitarian judge.

"Tradition." "State interest" is not the only common locution of American constitutional discourse that can have a misleadingly communitarian sound. "Tradition" is another. That word crops up mainly in the course of so-called modern substantive due process adjudication, stemming from the Supreme Court's invalidation, in 1965, of an anti-contraception law as an illicit deprivation of constitutionally guaranteed liberty.[107]

A word of explanation, now, of some constitutional-legal doctrine. Clauses in the Fifth and Fourteenth Amendments prohibit all governments in this country from making laws that "deprive any person of life, liberty, or property without due process of law." A long series of decisions has established that these prohibitions have some range of "substantive" application, meaning some range of application to laws that admittedly have been enacted and applied by constitutionally correct procedures, just because these laws are judged to trench unjustifiably on people's constitutionally valued interests in life or liberty or property. Substantive due process adjudication is "modern" when it focuses on such noneconomic aspects of liberty as sexual self-determination, family relationships, and control over one's physical destiny, as opposed to the economically significant contractual and occupational liberties to which the Supreme Court gave special protection in the decades prior to the New Deal.

All state "regulatory" laws—all laws that impose legal restrictions on conduct—impose some restriction on personal liberty, in the plainest possible sense of "liberty." They cannot all be unconstitutional. (Consider a law against murder.) The rule developed by the Supreme Court for such cases is that, ordinarily, the state need only cite some recognizably "rational" reason for the

---

[106] See William J. Brennan, Jr., "Address at the Dedication of the Samuel I. Newhouse Law Center," *Rutgers Law Review* 32 (1979): 173–83, 176–77.
[107] See Griswold v. Connecticut, 381 U.S. 479 (1965).

law in order to warrant its constitutionality, but that, in those exceptional cases where a state law trenches on "fundamental" aspects of liberty, a reviewing court will apply a more demanding test. The precise formulation of the stricter test appears to be in flux. Where "fundamental rights" are at stake, the Court has sometimes said that states must satisfy reviewing courts that their restrictive laws are "necessary" to the achievement of a "compelling" state interest that cannot adequately be served by any "less restrictive alternative." Recently, the Court has appeared to be moving to a test of whether the challenged state law imposes an "undue burden" on a constitutionally protected liberty.

As these differing tests have actually been carried out over the years, it has turned out that state regulatory laws almost never flunk the ordinary, "rational basis" test, but that they do quite often flunk the stricter "compelling interest" and "undue burden" tests reserved for laws that trench on fundamental rights. Obviously, then, the prevailing doctrine makes a great deal turn on the method used by the courts, led by the Supreme Court, to decide whether a given liberty or aspect of liberty—such as the freedom of persons in certain circumstances to act toward bringing their lives to an end without interference from the state—is "fundamental" and so protected by one of the stricter tests. It is in the Justices' debates over this question of classificatory method that their appeals to "tradition" have mainly occurred. Whether the aspect of liberty in question is a "fundamental" one, many opinions say, depends on how it has been regarded in a certain, historically identifiable "tradition."

"Tradition" has a vaguely communitarian ring about it. It seems that to accept tradition as an arbiter of normative disagreement is to subordinate one's own reason, judgment, or preference to the ways of the community taken whole. Justice Brennan often spoke of tradition. Sometimes, as we'll see, it was to scorn the use of tradition as a basis for constitutional-legal decision, or to warn against certain dangers involved in its use. Sometimes, though, Brennan called tradition to the support of his own arguments. Does that fact suggest communitarian tendencies in Justice

Brennan, or does it suggest caution about equating a judge's argumentative resort to the rhetoric of "tradition" with communitarian tendencies?

One can easily think of at least two good reasons for caution. The first is orthodoxy. For regular contributors to American constitutional debate, it is *de rigueur*, a mark of having the right stuff (much as, say, derision of political correctness would be for the *Crossfire* crowd) to aver that judges need more or less fixed and objective bases for their attributions of meanings to constitutional clauses, and moreover that those attributions must lie in a continuous line of refinement of relatively timeless basic principles of government that the people have always meant their Constitution to establish. Just mouthing the word "tradition" helps to keep up your standing, and that could be a major reason why some judges do it. (I don't mean by these remarks to suggest that a true traditionalist approach to constitutional interpretation lacks real bite or real merit, only that maybe not all judges really take its merits—whatever they may be—too much to heart.)

A second reason for caution is this: It would be one thing if judges never invoked tradition except as a reason for *denying* a claim for protection of individual liberty—thus deferring to a contrary desire ascribed to some community. That *does* reflect communitarian sensibilities, and it has in fact been the prevailing use of "tradition" in recent substantive due process disputation. Suspicions rise, though, when we see judges also, and it must be said with total ease, invoking "tradition" as an argument for expansive renderings of individual rights—with, of course, corresponding frustrations of competing desires (wills, judgments, values, understandings) ascribed to some community.

That is how Justice Brennan has used the notion of tradition, without significant exception.[108] For a plain example, we can recur

---

[108] The only conceivable exception that comes to mind is Roth v. United States, 354 U.S. 476 (1957), and it is not significant. In his opinion for the Court in *Roth*, Justice Brennan relied, in part, on the history of early American criminal-legal practice to establish that obscenity is "outside the protection intended for speech and press." Id. at 482–83. It was the Justice's first major pronounce-

to the *Cruzan* case.[109] One issue in the case was whether a person has a specially protected, "fundamental" liberty right to refuse medical treatment when it is certain that refusal will result directly in her death. Justice Brennan answered "yes," locating the right in "our common law tradition of medical self-determination." Using an oft-quoted formula from an opinion of Justice Cardozo, the Justice said the question was whether "freedom from unwanted medical treatment is . . . among those principles 'so rooted in the traditions and conscience of our people as to be ranked as fundamental.' "[110]

Judicial polemic has not been scrupulously consistent in its applications of the term "tradition." Sometimes, as when Justice Scalia invoked the spoils-system "tradition" in American politics to rebut a government worker's first-amendment claim against a partisan patronage dismissal,[111] the term evidently refers to what people in the relevant community have actually and regularly done, not to what they have reflectively approved as right or condemned as wrong. Sometimes, as when Justice Brennan invoked "the traditions and conscience of our people" to determine the fundamental status of the right to medical self-determination, "tradition" seems to refer to notions of right and wrong, or of rights and wrongs, that have been widely and reflectively held by the citizenry. Bridging these two usages is a third one that Justice Scalia came to advocate: "tradition" meaning a historical practice of granting legal recognition or protection to the specific aspect of liberty that is now being claimed as a strongly protected constitutional right.

---

ment after joining the Court, and it was to prove anomalous in his judicial work product. Indeed, he later retracted it. See Paris Adult Theatre I v. Slayton, 413 U.S. 49, 73–74 (1973) (Brennan, J., dissenting).

[109] 497 U.S. at 301 (Brennan, J., dissenting); see also Richmond Newspapers, Inc. v. Virginia, 448 U.S. 555, 589 (1980) (Brennan, J., concurring in the judgment) ("[T]he case for a right of access [to criminal trials] has special force when drawn from an enduring and vital tradition. . . .").

[110] *Cruzan* at 305 (quoting Snyder v. Massachusetts, 291 U.S. 97, 105 [1934]).

[111] See Rutan v. Republican Party, 497 U.S. 62, 92 (1990) (Scalia, J., dissenting).

Judicial disagreement over which "level" to look at—specific practices or general norms—tends to mirror disagreement between conservatives and liberals over the lessons to be drawn from "tradition" for purposes of the case at hand. Typically, what happens is this: One side says there has traditionally been a specific practice of P. P might, for example, be tax-supported religious chaplaincies in Congress and various state legislatures.[112] The other side says there has been a traditional commitment to general norm N. N could be the norm of church-state separation. (Another famous example: Americans committed themselves by the Fourteenth Amendment to equal protection of the laws, even as they were sending their children to racially segregated public schools.) Because in such cases the two sides are talking about different questions, it is perfectly possible that both sides are reporting accurately. If so, the proper direction of "tradition's" persuasive force will have to depend on some consideration other than reportorial accuracy. Other features of such disputes now heave into view. The content of N, the alleged general normative tradition, is always more abstract than that of P, the alleged specific practical tradition. In most cases, it will not be going too far to say that, relative to the P in the case at hand, the N might just as well be the general liberal norm of strong presumptive respect for individual liberty.

Regularly, when he was involved in such disputes, Justice Brennan's favored tradition was an N, and his N was a stalking horse for the general liberal value of liberty. Such an argumentative use of "tradition" is anti-communitarian, not communitarian. (There is, however, at least one case in which Justice Brennan might seem to have been brandishing a P, and we shall have to consider it.)[113]

"Tradition" as abstract libertarian norm. In *Elrod v. Burns* (1976),[114] Justice Brennan led a plurality of the Court in holding

---

[112] See Marsh v. Chambers, 463 U.S. 763 (1983).
[113] See Moore v. City of East Cleveland, discussed below.
[114] 427 U.S. 347 (1976).

that the First Amendment generally prohibits partisan patronage practices in public employment. In the later case of *Rutan v. Republican Party* (1990), a dissenting Justice Scalia, who had meanwhile come on the Court, raised against this doctrine the "landmark status" of patronage "as one of our accepted political traditions." "Such a venerable . . . tradition," Justice Scalia said in his deepest communitarian register, "is not to be laid on the examining table and scrutinized for its conformity to some abstract principle of First Amendment adjudication devised by this Court;" rather, the tradition is the very "stuff out of which" law is to be formed.[115] Justice Brennan did not deign to reply, perhaps because he had already made his response in *Elrod*:

> Our inquiry does not begin with the judgment of history, though the actual operation of a practice viewed in retrospect may help to assess its workings with respect to constitutional limitations. Compare *Brown v. Board of Education* with *Plessy v. Ferguson*. Rather inquiry must commence with identification of the constitutional limitations implicated by a challenged governmental practice.[116]

In *Rutan*, it fell to Justice Stevens to give the same point a bit more punch. "The tradition that is relevant in these cases," wrote Stevens, ironically and preposterously, "is the American commitment to examine and reexamine past and present practices against the basic principles embodied in the Constitution."[117]

Justice Brennan has not always been so curtly dismissive of tradition. Recall his dissenting opinion in *Michael H. v. Gerald D.*[118] As we saw, Justice Brennan did on that occasion expressly summon "tradition" to his aid. He did so, however, with explicit reservations, almost as if he dealt with the question of "tradition" only

[115] *Rutan* at 95–96 (Scalia, J., dissenting).
[116] *Elrod* at 354.
[117] *Rutan* at 92 (Stevens, J., concurring).
[118] Discussed in above, pp. 26–27.

under constraint of rhetorical fashion.[119] He took pains to explain why he would limit "tradition's" role in construing "the Constitution's capacious language." He warned against "seduction" by hopes that tradition could provide an objective demarcation of the bounds of constitutionally protected liberty. Such a hope, he said, must founder on controversy, not only about the specific contents of tradition's teachings for purposes of deciding the case at hand but, more fundamentally, about how to define the relevant *concept* of tradition. The concept itself, Justice Brennan said, is deeply contested with respect to such matters as whether to focus inquiry on specific practices or abstract norms, and how to tell when a tradition is long enough established (but not yet "too obsolete") to count in defining constitutionally protected liberty. Such ambiguities, the Justice said, render the concept "as malleable and elusive as the concept of liberty itself."[120]

None of this fazed Scalia. He answered that all of Brennan's problems could be easily solved by focusing inquiry on "the most specific level at which a relevant tradition protecting, or denying protection to, the asserted [liberty] right can be identified."[121] Accordingly, Scalia rejected Michael H.'s claim of a constitutionally

[119] Perhaps he saw no good escape from doing so. The liberty claimed by Michael H. was a liberty of association, specifically, with his daughter. Although the daughter's representative did in fact join Michael H. in seeking to have their relationship continued, see 491 U.S. at 114, this was not exactly a case of all parties to a voluntary association asserting individual liberties to choose their associates. Michael H. was certainly also pressing a claim to continue an association rooted in past events (his biological fathership of the child), not in unanimous choice. Moreover, his claim lacked obvious, strong foundation in actual relationship, Michael H. having actually been together with his daughter only during one or two months of her first year of life and some parts of an eight-month stretch of her third year. See id. at 113–15. In short, Michael H.'s case was not one he could count on winning by an appeal to unconjugated "liberty," a simple matter of the individual versus the state. Something more—something on the order of a particular normative "tradition"—was required to fit his claim into *fourteenth amendment* liberty. (Thanks to C. Edwin Baker for directing my notice to this feature of the case.)

[120] Michael H., 491 U.S. at 137, 138, 140 (Brennan, J., dissenting).

[121] See ibid., 127n. 6 (Scalia, J.).

protected right to associate with his child. He did so on the basis
of a "tradition" consisting of a negative concrete fact of legal history: that "persons in the situation of Michael H. and [the
child]"—that is, seeking legal recognition of their affiliation
against the contrary wishes of the mother and her husband—have
never "been treated as a protected family unit under the historic
practices of our society" and in fact "quite to the contrary our
traditions have protected the marital family . . . against the sort
of claim Michael asserts."[122]

As we saw, Brennan countered with the thought that Scalia had
addressed the question about tradition to the wrong object. For
Brennan, the pertinent tradition was that of respect for a cluster
of liberty interests including "freedom from physical restraint,
marriage, childbearing, childrearing," and unenumerated "others," and the decisive question was whether the parent-child relationship for which Michael H. sought protection belonged in all
reason to that cluster.

Robin West, a commentator sympathetic to Brennan, calls his
opinions in *Michael H.* and *Cruzan* regrettably conservative and
communitarian because they "derive the content of liberty . . .
from historical tradition" rather than directly "from liberal ideals." She means that these opinions purport to be based on slav-
ish-looking appeals to the "tradition" consisting of Warren and
Burger Court judicial precedent instead of on the Justice's own
freshly responsible (liberal) moral reading of the bill of rights.
West thinks it may have been pressure from "ideals of 'good'
judging"—a catering to public or peer expectations that judges
don't decide the law on their own hook but work at integrating
their decisions with the entire prior path of the law—that caused
these unfortunate desertions, or at any rate gestures of desertion,
by Brennan of reliance on his own best judgment of what "liberty"
means and requires.[123]

[122] Ibid., 124.
[123] Robin West, "The Ideal of Liberty: A Comment on *Michael H. v. Gerald
D.,*" *University of Pennsylvania Law Review* 139 (1991): 1373–91, at 1380,
1388–89.

Are we in topsy-turvydom, through the looking glass? Not exactly, but we do stand in a hall of mirrors. West's comment is shrewd. But West is also the theorist who suggested that the "privacy" and "autonomy" cases of the Warren and Burger Court years—the very ones from which Brennan mainly gathered up his "tradition" of liberty—are not a random or accidental lot, but rather a unified expression of a single principle, namely, the liberal's idea that "the ideal life must contain the power to make [personal] decisions independent of the community's moral beliefs."[124] In those terms, what Justice Brennan did in later cases such as *Cruzan* and *Michael H.* was nothing as simple as choosing "tradition" *in place of* "liberal ideals" as his guide to decision. It was to cast liberal ideals as *themselves* a tradition— as, indeed, *the* tradition that animates the corpus of "new" substantive due process cases (just as West says, only calling it not a tradition but an ideal), imparting to that corpus its character of integrity and consistency, of being "principled," as legal theorists say. That cuts the distinction between "tradition" and "principle" (or "ideals") pretty fine, in Brennan's particular case, although it doesn't answer West's particular objection to letting a reliance on facts of past practice intermediate rhetorically between a constitutional judge's ideals and his interpretations of the Constitution.

Justice Scalia's use of "tradition" (facts of specific past practices) in *Michael H.* was classically judicially "restrained." The Court, Scalia said, needs some securely objective way to "limit" the reach of substantive due process claims. In his view, an endlessly contestable, abstract notion of the "fundamentality" of this or that claimed liberty interest could not provide the needed limit, but facts of past practice could.[125] Justice Brennan's rejoinder was, by contrast, characteristically judicial activist, presumably more to the taste of Professor West. It was the rejoinder of the committed

---

[124] Robin West, "Progressive and Conservative Constitutionalism," *Michigan Law Review* 88 (1990): 641–721, at 702.

[125] Ibid., 122.

moral reader. "The document that the plurality construes today," Brennan wrote,

> is not the living charter that I have taken to be the Constitution; it is instead a stagnant, hidebound, archaic document steeped in the prejudices and superstitions of a long time past. *This* Constitution does not recognize that times change, does not see that sometimes a practice or rule outlives its foundations.[126]

Scalia's argument from tradition was not only judicially restrained. It was also outspokenly solidarist, communitarian, and social-conservative. It proceeded, as he said, from a belief that the purpose of the Constitution's Due Process Clauses is not to "enable this Court to invent new [values]," but to "prevent future generations from lightly casting aside important traditional values."[127] (Held by whom or what? The moral sovereignty of the communal agent just goes without saying here.) Justice Brennan's bias, by contrast, was characteristically cultural pluralist and social-critical: "We are not an assimilative, homogeneous society," Justice Brennan said,

> but a facilitative, pluralistic one, in which we must be willing to abide someone else's unfamiliar or even repellent practice because the same tolerant impulse protects our own idiosyncracies. . . . In a community such as ours, "liberty" must include the freedom not to conform. [Justice Scalia's opinion] . . . squashes this freedom by requiring specific approval from history before protecting anything in the name of liberty.[128]

Regard for community (without communitarianism). At issue in *Moore v. City of East Cleveland*[129] was a zoning ordinance that reserved certain areas of the city for single family residential uses

---

126 Ibid., 141.
127 Ibid. at 122n. 2 (Scalia, J.).
128 Ibid. at 141 (Brennan, J., dissenting).
129 431 U.S. 494 (1977).

and then defined "family" in a way that, broadly speaking, allowed only for nuclear and not extended family living. The petitioner in the case was an African-American homeowner, Inez Moore, in whose house were living one son of hers and two grandsons. One of the grandsons was the son of the resident son, the other was the resident son's nephew. It was the presence of the nephew that the zoning ordinance made unlawful.

Justice Brennan joined Justice Powell's controlling opinion, which applied the constitutional protection of liberty to prevent East Cleveland, in Powell's memorable phrase, from "standardizing" its residents by "forcing all to live in certain narrowly defined family patterns."[130] Justice Brennan also added his own separate opinion—one that speaks of both tradition and group identities. "I write," he said,

> to underscore the cultural myopia of the . . . ordinance . . . in light of the tradition of the American home that has been a feature of our society since our beginning as a Nation— the "tradition" in the Court's words, "of uncles, aunts, cousins and especially grandparents sharing a household along with parents and children. . . ." The line drawn by this ordinance displays depressing insensitivity toward the economic and emotional needs of a very large part of our society.
>
> . . . The Constitution cannot be interpreted . . . to tolerate the imposition by government upon the rest of us of white suburbia's preference in patterns of family living.
>
> . . . [T]he prominence of other than nuclear families among ethnic and racial minority groups, including our black citizens, surely demonstrates that the "extended family" pattern remains a vital tenet of our society. . . . [I]n prohibiting this pattern of family living . . ., appellee city has chosen a device that deeply intrudes into family associational rights that historically have been central, and today remain central, to a large portion of our population.[131]

[130] Ibid. at 506.
[131] Ibid. at 507–10 (Brennan, J., concurring).

Brennan further suggested that the extended-family living pattern adopted by African-Americans was at least in part a result of "economic necessity" and a desire for "economic and social support" experienced by people establishing "beachheads" in a strange or hostile land.[132]

Without a doubt, Brennan's *Moore* opinion gives normative weight to interests he perceives people to have in adhering to the special cultural understandings and practices of self-conscious social groups. That does not make his opinion into a communitarian document by my definition, and in fact the opinion proves upon examination to be much closer to libertarian in spirit.

Against a communitarian reading of Justice Brennan's *Moore* opinion stands a difficulty adduced by Robert Burt in his critical commentary on the *Moore* case:[133] the most salient, organized, and articulate community in *Moore* is the losing party, the City of East Cleveland. Not every city deserves to count as a community in every case, but there may be reason to say that in this case East Cleveland did. As Justice Brennan's opinion pointed out (citing the fact as a reason why he did not ascribe any racially discriminatory intention to the East Cleveland ordinance), East Cleveland was a predominantly black city whose city manager and city commission were black.[134]

The Powell opinion that Brennan joined used the rhetorical device of first pretending to suppose the city's ordinance aimed at avoiding humdrum evils like traffic congestion and crowding, then proceeding to blast it for its obvious ill-suitedness to such aims.[135] Professor Burt credits East Cleveland's lawmakers with greater competence. He surmises that the motivations behind the East Cleveland ordinance were not blunderingly environmental and managerial but quite adeptly cultural and self-expressive: to define the city as a "socially and economically upwardly mobile"

---

[132] Ibid. at 508–9 (Brennan, J., concurring).
[133] Robert A. Burt, "The Constitution of the Family," *Supreme Court Review* 1979: 329–95, at 388–91.
[134] See ibid. at 510.
[135] Ibid., 499–500.

community; to align it with the "more prevalent American tradition of nuclear family households . . . bonded in an extended communal group linked by shared social identity;" and to do this in considered and declared renunciation of "the ghetto lifestyle."[136] In other words: the city, like the state in Rehnquist's *Cruzan* opinion, aims to sustain for itself a certain, majority-preferred ethical climate.

A communitarian judge is the one who would have seen the ordinance as Professor Burt sees it, and for that reason given it the benefit of any constitutional doubt. A communitarian judge would have regarded East Cleveland as itself a claimant to freedom. He would have said that local communities, at least when like-minded ones do not monopolize the regional living space for their particular ethical and lifestyle preferences, have their own rights not to be "standardized" by gospel civil libertarianism, their own rights not to be pressed into the grid of legal restraints devised for governments of country-sized American states.[137] Justice Brennan, to the contrary, took the liberal individualist position. The Constitution, he chided, does not allow a city government to impose on its diverse population the particular preference of "white suburbia" regarding family living patterns.[138] But then what is the point of his opinion's salute to an American subcultural tradition of extended family living? We have to read that as Brennan's way of saying that the individual claimant, Inez Moore, did indeed have at stake in this case a substantial and indeed a "fundamental" sort of liberty interest—that she was not a rebel without a cause, stubbornly and for no fair reason refusing some routine, inevitable inconvenience of membership in a legally ordered society. At the end of the day, "tradition" has dropped out as an independent, load-bearing part of Justice Bren-

---

[136] Burt, "Constitution of the Family," 389–90.

[137] See Gerald E. Frug, *"Cities and Homeowners' Associations: A Reply,"* *University of Pennsylvania Law Review* 130 (1982): 1589–1601, at 1599–1601; Gerald E. Frug, "The City As a Legal Concept," *Harvard Law Review* 93 (1980): 1057–1154, at 1076–78.

[138] Ibid., 508.

nan's constitutional-legal argument. Its appearance in his opinion
is sheer rhetoric.

Professor Burt, the true communitarian in this dialogue, makes
the point that Inez Moore could probably have moved her household to almost any other greater Cleveland location and not run
into a similarly bothersome zoning restriction (East Cleveland's
was highly unusual), but when she won her case "the nuclear families that had come together in East Cleveland could find nowhere
to remain together as a self-consciously contained community."
Thus, "victory for Mrs. Moore was total defeat for the other residents of East Cleveland, while victory for them was not total defeat for her. . . ."[139] It is not hard to imagine Justice Brennan's
liberal-minded response. It would have been that, in conditions
of social visionary conflict over mores and lifestyles, no contender
ought to go armed with the weaponry of state coercion. It was,
after all "the imposition *by government* . . . of white suburbia's
preference in patterns of living" that the Justice said the Constitution will not abide.[140]

No doubt Brennan would have granted what logic compels.
Sometimes, groups of individuals share a wish to maintain a certain special ambience and ethos in "their" corner of the world. If
constitutional law dictates that such groups must be stripped of
the regulatory weapon whenever its use infringes on claims of
others to private liberty and autonomy, then the law will often
put the members of these groups at a severe disadvantage as
against the rugged individualists who don't give a hoot for what
happens next door. That is, to be sure, a hard consequence of
Brennan's liberal-not-communitarian position in the *Moore* case.
Whether Brennan's acceptance of that consequence warrants
Burt's charge against him of "insensitivity" to the East Cleveland

---

[139] Burt, "Constitution of the Family," 390–91.

[140] Cf. West, "Progressive and Conservative Constitutionalism" ("Classical
liberals, far more than modern conservatives, distrust centralized power of *any*
sort . . . . [They] require the state, whenever possible, to defer to the normative
authority of the smallest unit of power—*individuals*—and then to promote that
normative authority through noninterference.")

majority's "economic and emotional needs"[141] is hard to say. To rate a (communitarian) value below where you rate a conflicting or competing (liberal) value does not necessarily show your insensitivity to the first value. It might simply show your commitment to prefer a competing principle when the two, regrettably, come into conflict. It might reflect a hard but inescapable choice We shall have more to say about this soon.

To this point in our review, Justice Brennan does not sound terribly much like a communitarian. Yet the Justice did plainly appreciate the central place in human life of familial and other group attachments and relationships, and he sometimes gave that consideration decisive weight in his judgments. In *Bowen v. Gilliard* (1987),[142] the Supreme Court upheld against substantive due process attack a statute that had the effect of forcing certain children to choose between leaving their mother's household and care and losing a support relationship with their father. (The factual and legal situation in *Gilliard* was intricate and bizarre. I summarize it in the note.)[143] Justice Brennan, dissenting, said

---

[141] Burt, "Constitution of the Family," 390–91.

[142] 483 U.S. 587, 609 (1987) (Brennan, J., dissenting).

[143] A child, *C*, lives with one parent (typically his mother) while receiving all the money required for his support from his nonresident father, who pays either voluntarily or under legal compulsion. Also living with the mother are her other children, for the support of whom she receives a federal welfare allowance computed on the basis of the number of children she supports. The mother, father, and *C* are all perfectly content to let *C* be disregarded in calculating the mother's household's federal allowance. The government, however, is not content. The law challenged in *Gilliard* provides that as long as *C* lives in the mother's household, *C* must assign over to the government the right to any money his father might pay to him in excess of $50 per month; in exchange, *C* will be counted among the household's dependents in computing the federal allowance. For some families, the law's practical effect, in all likelihood neither contemplated nor desired by the drafters of the law, is this: if *C* wishes to continue receiving support from his father, he must move from the mother's household and care. Should *C* choose against such a move, then the government's requirement will be financially disadvantageous to the hard-pressed family, because (but for the legal requirement in question) the father's monthly payments would have exceeded by more than $50 the increment to the mother's welfare allowance that results from adding *C* to her family unit. In that case the law also, obviously,

that a law imposing such a choice violates the fundamental aspect of constitutional liberty that the Court had previously recognized as " 'freedom of personal choice in matters of family life . . .' "[144] Here is how he explained the fundamental character of the relational interests at stake—not only the child's, but the father's too:

> The [father's] . . . provision of support . . . constitutes a parent-child relationship founded upon the pledge of the father to provide support . . . responsive to the needs of the unique child that is the father's own. . . . [A]side from its intrinsic importance, child support is a strand tightly interwoven with other forms of connection between father and child. Removal of this strand can unravel all the others.[145]

In *Moore*, Justice Brennan stood opposed to the coercive enactment by government of a particular ethical or lifestyle norm that a majority of local residents preferred. In *Gilliard*, he stood opposed to a governmental imposition of compulsion upon members of a family to destroy or deplete their community and to accept a dependency upon the state in place of family-provided support. One decision overrides a communitarian value, the other protects such a value, but of course there is no problem of inconsistency between the two: obviously, both protect individual or private liberty over governmental compulsion. Brennan made that clear enough:

---

leaves the father with no reason under the sun to continue making voluntary support payments to his child. If the father is making the payments under obligation of contract or family court order, then the effect is still to sever that strand of the parent-child (father-*C*) relation consisting of the father's paying support money to *C*; the father continues to pay, but now he pays to the government and not to *C*. Thus the law forces *C* to a choice from which there is no escape without rupture of familial relationships. *C* can choose to part from Mom in order to retain a support relationship with Dad, or *C* stay with Mom and lose Dad's support.

[144] Ibid. at 611–12 (Brennan, J., dissenting) (quoting Santosky v. Kramer, 455 U.S. 632, 639 [1974]).

[145] Ibid. at 616–17.

If we are far removed from the Platonic Republic, it is because our commitment to diversity and decentralized human relationships has made us attentive to the danger of Government intrusion on private life. Those who are affected by the Government in this case are fathers and children who have sustained a relationship whereby the child is supported by the father, not dependent on the State. The State has told the child that if it is to live with a mother not so fortunate, it too must become a dependent of the State. If it does so, the child's material needs will no longer be met by a father's attention to his particular child. Rather, the child will be one of many who are supported by the Government, and the father, powerless to direct assistance to his child, can only reimburse the Government for supporting the entire household. Such an arrangement calls to mind Aristotle's criticism of the family in Plato's Republic: "[E]ach citizen will have a thousand sons: they will not be the sons of each citizen individually: any and every son will be equally the son of any and every father; and the result will be that every son will be equally neglected by every father." (*The Politics of Aristotle* 44 [E. Barker trans., 1958])[146]

A trickier question of consistency is presented by *Corporation of Presiding Bishop v. Amos* (1987).[147] In that Establishment Clause case, Justice Brennan allowed a regard for facts of human sociality to carve a unique exception into his usually severe stance against the permissibility of lawmaking that responds specifically to the interests of religion.[148] He concurred in upholding an exemption

---

[146] *Gilliard*, 483 U.S. at 632–33.

[147] 483 U.S. 327, 340 (Brennan, J., concurring in the judgment).

[148] See, e.g., Marsh v. Chambers, 463 U.S. 783, 795 (1983) (Brennan, J., dissenting from a decision permitting a tax-payed Christian chaplaincy in a state legislature); Lynch v. Donnelly, 465 U.S. 668, 694 (1984) (Brennan, J., dissenting from a decision permitting a crèche display on public lands); Edwards v. Aguillard, 482 U.S. 578 (1987) (Brennan, J.) (applying strict antiestablishment doctrine to prohibit Louisiana from regulating the content of public school science teaching); cf. id. 610, 634 (Scalia, J., dissenting) (attributing Brennan's deci-

for religiously sponsored non-profit organizations from fair-employment laws prohibiting religion-based discrimination in hiring. He did so despite his recognition that the exemption can result in severe burdens on the religious liberties of individuals, by making them choose between religious conformity—perhaps even pretended religious conformity—and unemployment. The resulting "potential for coercion," he wrote, "is in serious tension with our commitment to individual freedom of conscience."[149]

Brennan nevertheless concluded that the exemption was constitutionally defensible because it was also protective of the religious liberties of individuals, none of whom can practice a religion alone, all of whom can only do so as members of a company of believers:

> Religion includes important communal elements for most believers. . . . For many individuals, religious activity derives meaning in large measure from participation in a larger religious community. Such a community represents an ongoing tradition of shared belief, an organic entity not reducible to a mere aggregate of individuals. Determining that certain activities are in furtherance of an organization's religious mission, and that only those committed to that mission should conduct them, is thus a means by which a religious community defines itself. Solicitude for a church's ability to do so reflects the idea that furtherance of the autonomy of religious organizations often furthers individual religious freedom as well.
>
> The authority to engage in this process of self-definition inevitably involves what we normally regard as infringement on free exercise rights, since a religious organization is able to condition employment in certain activities on subscription

---

sion to "an instinctive reaction that any governmentally imposed requirements upon the teaching of evolution must be a manifestation of Christian fundamentalist repression" and asserting that "the people of Louisiana, including those who are Christian fundamentalists, are . . . entitled to [demand] that . . . evidence against evolution [be] presented in their schools").

[149] *Amos* at 340 (Brennan, J., concurring in the judgment).

to particular religious tenets. We are willing to countenance the imposition of such a condition because we deem it vital that, if certain activities constitute part of a religious community's practice, then a religious organization should be able to require that only members of its community perform those activities.[150]

Any lawyer can see ways to distinguish the cases of *Amos* and *Moore*, but when you set up the *Amos* case as Brennan at one point perhaps carelessly did, as presenting "a confrontation between the rights of religious organizations and those of individuals,"[151] then clear parallels between that case and *Moore* are impossible to overlook. In both cases, a superior governmental authority decides that a certain class of lower-level social organizations should, for reasons of human interest, be allowed to exercise certain powers of corporate self-determination, despite resulting infringements on important aspects of the liberties of some individuals. In *Amos*, the superior authority is Congress, the class of lower-level organizations is churches, the powers are those of choosing contractual associates (employees) with a free hand, and the individual liberties that have to be forgone are liberties of religious conscience, although of persons who can seek employment elsewhere. In *Moore*, the superior authority is the state of Ohio (the source of the law that empowered Ohio cities to legislate as East Cleveland did), the class of lower-level organizations is cities, the powers are those of protecting quality of life through control over land uses, and the individual liberties infringed are those of family and household formation, although by persons who can seek location elsewhere.

In *Moore*, Brennan found that the Constitution required deference to the rights of individuals despite resulting cost to the concerns of an organized group. In *Amos*, he found that it did not. Reading the Justice's opinions in the two cases, it's hard not to get the sense of a real difference in the degrees of sympathy Bren-

---

[150] Ibid. at 342–43.
[151] Ibid. at 340.

nan was able to muster for the interests and stakes of individual constituents in the law's treatment of their group. In *Amos*, he sympathized; in *Moore*, he did not. Professor Burt's comment begins to bite.

There remains, however, a glaring difference between the two cases. The "organization" in *Moore* was itself an arm of government, entrusted by the state with a share of the latter's monopoly of lawful force for purposes only of the common good of residents, whereas the "organization" in *Amos* was privately formed and maintained for the voluntary pursuit of particular chosen aims of its membership. In prevailing American constitutional doctrine and tradition, that "public/private" distinction easily provides a basis for treating the two cases differently. Granted, Justice Brennan was not himself one who could or did approve a mechanistic approach to deciding who or what should be regarded as exercising "state" powers covered by the restraints of the Bill of Rights.[152] but neither did he ever propose to jettison entirely the distinction in constitutional law between private action and "state action," nor could he have done so consistently with his liberalism. The fact that cities exercise powers of governmental command whereas churches do not must surely figure in any explanation of Brennan's joint positions in *Amos* and *Moore*.

But Professor Burt is not wholly off the mark, either. If one were the "romantic" liberal I read Justice Brennan to have been, one would especially resist governmental dictation of mores when the dictates in question seem woodenly imitative of fashion set by society's dominant or privileged strata ("white suburbia"). Justice Brennan's political thought was surely shaped to a considerable degree by distinctions he thought he could draw between domi-

---

[152] Cf., e.g., DeShaney v. Winnebago County Dep't of Social Services, 489 U.S. 189, 204 (1989) (Brennan, J., dissenting); San Francisco Arts & Athletics, Inc. v. United States Olympic Committee, 482 U.S. 522 (1987) (Brennan, J., dissenting); Jackson v. Metropolitan Edison Co., 419 U.S. 345, 179 (1974) (Brennan, J., dissenting); Moose lodge No. 107 v. Irvis, 407 U.S. 163, 184 (1972) (Brennan, J., dissenting).

nation and insurgency, fashion and critique. He was, as we have seen and are about to see again, anything but hostile to insurgent and critical cultural contestation. But contestation would have gone off the rails, in his view, when it took the form of subjecting dissenters to the tastes and values of a social group strong enough to take the reins of government, even if only local.

EQUALITY, GROUPS, AND POSITIVE SOCIAL RIGHTS

Individual Liberty and the Role of the State

Charles Fried—Justice of the Massachusetts Supreme Judicial Court, ex-Solicitor-General of the United States, and no friend to group rights—offers the following account of a "group-rights perspective":

> [It] sees groups—ethnic, cultural, gender—as having a status independent of and even superior to that of individual group members. It assigns a value to the well-being of the group that is similarly independent of and perhaps superior to that of its component members. From this view it follows that government policy should measure benefits and burdens in terms of groups and, when equality is the issue, emphasize equality between groups as such.[153]

Fried thinks that Justice Brennan's treatment of race-discrimination claims under the Constitution, and particularly his complex response to complaints of "reverse discrimination," involved him in the promotion of group rights.[154] I do not.

Brennan certainly did maintain that active governmental concern with group representation is sometimes constitutionally justifiable. He did not, however, derive that conclusion from anything like assignment of an independent and overriding value to

[153] Fried, "*Metro Broadcasting*," 109–10.
[154] See ibid., 109, 125, 127.

the well-being of any group *qua* group; he derived it, as we'll see, from a concern about justice for individuals and a respect for everyone's interest in freedom. But now comes a crucial point. Brennan was a liberal. He was also a social democrat. His conception of individual liberty and the social conditions of its nurturance was not the Spencerian ideal of the individual self-sufficiently independent of society and state.[155] In Brennan's view, hands-off detachment and neglect of the social arena were not always signs of constitutional virtue in a government supposedly dedicated to respect for every individual. When he spoke of " 'the protection of the dignity of the human being and the recognition that every individual has fundamental rights which government cannot deny him,' "[156] he meant rights including positive claims to aid and protection, and to a governmentally active "adjustment of restraints" as required to realize true "liberty of opportunity" for all.[157]

In holding that a state could not remove a person from the welfare rolls without first giving that person a face-to-face hearing, Brennan cited "the Nation's [founding] commitment . . . to foster the dignity and well-being of all persons within its borders."[158] In protest against the Court's conclusion that a state has no constitutionally mandated duty to protect a child from physical abuse by a parent, Brennan derided the notion that "the Constitution does not establish positive rights."[159] Such views well become a judge for whom political freedom meant unprejudiced, emancipated access for all to the contestations of democratic pub-

---

[155] See, e.g., Herbert Spencer, *The Man Versus the State* (London: Williams & Norgate, 1884).

[156] Nat Hentoff, "Profiles: The Constitutionalist," *New Yorker*, March 12, 1990, 45 (quoting Justice Brennan's words in a 1987 television interview).

[157] See Brennan, *Reason, Passion*, 965–70, 974–75 (1987), quoting Benjamin N. Cardozo, *The Paradoxes of Legal Science* (New York: Columbia University Press, 1928), 118.

[158] Goldberg v. Kelly, 397 U.S. 254, 264–65 (1970).

[159] DeShaney v. Dep't of Social Services, 489 U.S. 189, 205 (Brennan, J., dissenting).

lic life.[160] Unmistakably at the core of Justice Brennan's constitutional theory is commitment to "a society in which personal liberty is sacred."[161] "Sacred" means inviolate; it does not mean untainted by any support from government action.

Affirmative Action

Adjudicating the constitutionality of allegedly "benign" legal classifications by race and sex could never have been untroubled work for Justice Brennan and others, such as Blackmun, Marshall, and White, with whom he was generally allied when he supported such classifications. These men never, after all, surrendered their alliance with the country's "deep belief" that differences in legal treatments of persons should always reflect differences in personal "responsibility" or "merit" and not "immutable characteristic[s] which [their] possessor[s] are powerless to escape or set aside."[162] They knew, too, that they had to reckon with complexities surrounding group-based legal preferences, starting with the difficulty of isolating the use of preferences to disrupt structures and cycles of social stratification from their use in mindless repetition of those same cycles and structures.[163] That is why Justices

[160] See above, pp. 68–71.

[161] Dorsen, *Justice Brennan Deserves Better Treatment*, Nat'l L. J., March 2, 1987, at 13, 46.

[162] *Bakke*, 438 U.S. 360–61; see also Metro Broadcasting, Inc. v. FCC, 497 U.S. 547, 564–65 (1990) (Brennan, J.) (reaffirming the need for special judicial scrutiny of "benign race-conscious measures" that are not "designed to compensate victims of past governmental or societal discrimination"); City of Richmond v. J. A. Croson Co., 488 U.S. 469, 535, 537, 559 (1989) (Marshall, J., joined by Brennan and Blackmun, JJ., dissenting) (finding Richmond's minority set-aside program for city contracts justified by the " 'important governmental objectives' " of "eradicating the effects of past discrimination" and "preventing the city's own spending decisions from reinforcing and perpetuating the exclusionary effects of past discrimination" [quoting *Bakke* at 359 (Brennan, White, Marshall, and Blackmun, JJ., concurring in the judgment in part and dissenting in part)]).

[163] See, e.g., *Bakke*, 438 U.S. at 360 (Brennan, White, Marshall, and Blackmun, JJ., concurring in the judgment in part and dissenting in part) ("While a carefully tailored statute designed to remedy past discrimination could avoid

Brennan and Marshall, especially, were tough and relentless critics of ostensibly "preferential" treatment for women.[164] It is why
they saw fit to treat the histories of race and sex in American
society as each presenting a distinct problem of constitutional
analysis.

In its fully matured form, Brennan's doctrine on racial preferences consisted of the following propositions: (1) In contemporary American society, individuals often are socially identified,
and many identify themselves, by perceived facts of membership
in color and/or national-origin groups. This is in part a matter of
how persons are perceived and identified by others, in part a matter of how they understand themselves.[165] (2) The presumptive
constitutional right of an individual not to be denied an advantage
by government by reason of race or sex may sometimes be over-
ridden by competing considerations.[166] (3) The overriding considerations may include correction for a past history of societal
discrimination against persons of color.[167] (4) The overriding considerations may also include "forward-looking" policies such as
ensuring diversity of viewpoints in various social settings.[168] (5)
Securing the presence in various arenas of public life—work-

[the] vices [of stigmatizing all members of the beneficiary class with a badge of
inferiority] the line between honest and thoughtful appraisal of the effects of
past discrimination and paternalistic stereotyping is not so clear.").

[164] See, e.g., Craig v. Boren, 429 U.S. 190 (1976) (Brennan J.); Califano v.
Goldfarb, 430 U.S. 199 (1977) (plurality opinion) (Brennan, J.); Weinberger v.
Wiesenfeld, 420 U.S. 636 (1975) (Brennan, J.); Schlesinger v. Ballard, 419 U.S.
498, 511 (1975) (Brennan, J., dissenting); Kahn v. Shevin, 416 U.S. 351, 360
(1974) (Brennan, J., dissenting). See also Califano v. Webster, 430 U.S. 313
(1977) (per curiam) (expressly hinging a sex-based statutory classification's validity on a specific judicial determination, after searching scrutiny, that the classification was genuinely compensatory and free of stigmatic motivation and meaning).

[165] See, e.g., City of Richmond v. J. A. Croson Co., 488 U.S. 469, 534–39
(1989) (Marshall, J., joined by Brennan and Blackmun, JJ., dissenting); cf.
McCleskey v. Kemp, 481 U.S. 279, 321–28 (1987) (Brennan, J., dissenting).

[166] See, e.g., *Bakke*, 438 U.S. at 355–59 (Brennan, White, Marshall, and Blackmun, JJ., concurring in the judgment in part and dissenting in part).

[167] See, e.g., ibid. at 365–66, 369.

[168] See, e.g., *Metro Broadcasting* at 564–65.

places, professions, broadcast media—of representative numbers (I use the term loosely) of members of historically subordinated racial and national-origin groups is itself a legitimate goal for government and can sometimes justify the use of a racial preference.[169] (6) A racial preference, therefore, may sometimes be justified although it is not designed to confine its benefits to victims, or its burdens to perpetrators, of specifically identified past discrimination.[170]

The question I want to consider here is not whether any or all of the practices that the foregoing premises might justify as constitutionally permissible are wise or desirable as social policy. (To my mind, some would be, some wouldn't, and the judgments required are often fiendishly hard, open to sincere disagreement among people sharing very similar visions of the good society.) It is whether there is anything about the premises that is either logically incompatible with liberal individualism (for example, one or more of them reflects a strong communitarian belief in group consciousness or group agency) or is otherwise morally repellent from a liberal-individualist point of view.

Suppose the aims of your practice are sturdily liberal-individualist, inspired by a universalistic regard for everyone's individuality and for the liberties and opportunities of everyone. In considering what it would be reasonable to do in pursuit of such aims, you run into certain facts (as you take them to be) about the communal bases of individual identities. Your recognition of these facts does not in any way contradict your *normative* individualism. As a normative individualist, you insist that each person leads a singular life, a life of his or her own, and that each one's life is a singular focus of moral concern. Singularity of a life, however, does not mean the life is rootless, solitary, or self-sufficient. There is no need to conceive of a singular and singularly valued self as "prior to" or separate from its "ends,"[171] no reason why such a

---

[169] Ibid., 571; *Bakke* at 366.

[170] See, e.g., *Bakke*, 438 U.S. at 365–66.

[171] Cf. Michael Sandel, *Liberalism and the Limits of Justice* (Cambridge: Cambridge University Press,1982), 54–59, discussing a remark in John Rawls, *A The-*

self may not be socially situated, culturally constructed, and biographically encumbered. There is no reason why singular and singularly valued persons may not be capable of knowing goods in common that they cannot know alone.[172] There is not even any reason why the singularly valued self-consciousness of every individual may not depend on the ways in which persons reciprocally recognize each other in society.

All these social dimensions of personality, that there is no need or reason for a normative individualist to reject, are ones—let us say—that you in fact believe are widely true of persons in our society. You therefore have to face the question of whether or when it becomes illiberal—a break with the liberal commitments you claim to hold—to take the facts of human sociality into consideration when deciding what are correct or acceptable governmental practices. There may well be such a point. A liberal might certainly hold to a certain anthropological belief while concluding that it would sometimes or often disserve liberal aims to use that belief as a premise for social policy or legal doctrine. The point, however, cannot plausibly lie at zero. The liberal faith cannot plausibly demand absolute, flat refusal of all recognition in social policy of the social, group-affiliative components of personality and identity. It is not credible to say that the frontiers of liberalism are crossed just as soon as someone argues that people's self-attributed or other-attributed affiliation with a race or color group contributes to their social identity in ways that crucially govern the effects of a given law or social practice on their freedom or well-being as individuals. To say *that* would be to say, for example, that denouncing affirmative action because it stigmatizes persons of color is illiberal—which is not a plausible construal of liberalism in contemporary American constitutional debate.[173]

---

ory of Justice (Cambridge, Mass.: Harvard University Press, 1971), at 560 ("The self is prior to the ends which are affirmed by it.").

[172] Cf. Sandel, *Liberalism*, 183 ("[W]hen politics goes well, we can know a good in common that we cannot know alone.").

[173] See, e.g., Charles Fried, *Order and Law: Arguing the Reagan Revolution: A First-Hand Account* (New York: Simon & Schuster, 1991), 99–100.

The question, then, must be whether Justice Brennan's views on racial preferences conceived the facts of racial-group affiliation, or reasoned from them, in ways that deviate notably from a liberal standpoint. Here it will serve clarity to divide the inquiry. We shall first put that question to the Justice's approval (in *Bakke*, for example) of correction for past, general societal discrimination as a constitutionally acceptable justification for race-based preferences. Then we shall put it to his approval (in *Metro Broadcasting*) of "diversity" as such a justification.

Correcting for past societal discrimination. In *Bakke*, a case involving use of a racial preference in medical school admissions, Justice Brennan joined three colleagues in asserting the constitutional legitimacy of measures designed "to achieve minority participation in previously segregated areas of public life."[174] In the context of the *Bakke* case, that meant "participation" in (broadly speaking) representative numbers. This remark in *Bakke* is the closest Justice Brennan has come to expressly fixing on the status or success of a group as such as an ultimate aim for social policy or governmental action. But it doesn't come very close (especially when read in light of the committed individualism of the speaker's political doctrine at large), because it speaks to a matter that bears directly on fairness to individuals.

Individuals' prospects and opportunities may be strongly affected by "statistical discrimination" in various fields of endeavor. As Cass Sunstein once spelled out the argument:

> It is a mistake to take productivity within any social group as static or unaffected by employer decisions. Such decisions . . . [affect how people] choose to invest in human capital. Decisions about education, child care, training, drug use, employment programs, and tradeoffs between work and leisure will be affected by patterns of discrimination. In a market having such discrimination, . . . lower [human capital] investments [on the part of members of disadvantaged groups] are perfectly rational. As market actors, women

---

[174] See *Bakke*, 438 U.S. at 366.

should invest less than men in training to be (for example) pilots . . . if [this profession discriminates] against women and thus reward[s] their investment less than that of men.

The result will often be a vicious circle or even a spiral. Because of existing discrimination, the relevant groups will [rationally] invest less in human capital; because of this lower investment, the discrimination will persist or perhaps increase as its statistical rationality itself increases; because of this effect, investments will decrease still further, and so on.

An additional problem is that private preferences, of both discriminators and their victims, tend to adapt to the status quo, and to do so in such a way as to make significant change harder to achieve. . . . The victims of inequality tend to reduce dissonance by adapting their preferences to the available opportunities. . . . Or people may adapt their aspirations to the persistent and often irrationally held belief that the world is in fact just. The beneficiaries of the status quo tend to do the same, concluding that the victims deserve their fate, that they are responsible for it, or that the current situation is part of an intractable, given, or natural order.

[T]hese effects [reinforce each other] in potentially powerful ways. If there is ordinary prejudice, it will interact with statistical discrimination to produce more of both. People tend to notice events consistent with their prejudices and to disregard events that are inconsistent with them, thus resulting in more prejudice and more statistical discrimination. Employers will hire fewer members of disadvantaged groups, who will in turn appear less frequently in desirable positions, with consequent reinforcing effects on both prejudice and statistical discrimination.[175]

Sunstein would appear to be speaking a plain enough sort of truth. Here is a random bit of evidence of how widespread among us are the intuitions to which he is giving expression. In the course

[175] Cass R. Sunstein, "Three Civil Rights Fallacies," *California Law Review* 79 (1991): 751–74, at 758–59, 761.

of laying down a strong constitutional presumption against racial preferences in her *Croson* opinion, Justice O'Connor speculatively explained the low representation of blacks among building contractors in the Richmond area (which she refused to accept as significant proof of racial discrimination by anyone) by raising the possibility that blacks just don't find the construction business attractive relative to other business opportunities. "There are," she offered, "numerous explanations for this dearth of minority participation, including past societal discrimination in education and economic opportunities as well as both black and white career and entrepreneurial choices. Blacks may be disproportionately attracted to industries other than construction."[176] O'Connor didn't suggest any further explanation (other than, implicitly, the souls of black folk) for that last bit of armchair sociology. O'Connor is not a racist. What could she have been thinking?

In an argument running somewhat parallel to Sunstein's, Kimberlé Crenshaw has focused more on what she calls "ordinary prejudice":

> Believing that Blacks are inferior and that the economy impartially rewards the superior over the inferior, whites see that most Blacks are indeed worse off than whites are, which reinforces their sense [both] that the market is operating [impartially] . . . [and] that Blacks are *indeed* inferior. After all, equal opportunity *is* the rule and the market *is* an impartial judge; if Blacks are on the bottom it must reflect their relative inferiority. . . . Racism, combined with equal opportunity mythology, provides a rationalization for oppression, making it difficult for whites to see the Black situation as illegitimate or unnecessary.[177]

Arguments like these have venerable liberal credentials, for example in the celebrated writing of Gunnar Myrdal and his associ-

---

[176] See *Croson*, 488 U.S. at 503.

[177] Kimberlé Williams Crenshaw, "Race, Reform, and Retrenchment: Transformation and Legitimation in Antidiscrimination Law," Harvard Law Review 101 (1988): 1331–87, at 1380.

ates.[178] Nothing in Justice Brennan's defenses of discrimination-correcting affirmative action asserts, implies, or requires appeal to anything further out on the road to Bosnia. If you grant their sociological premises, then Myrdal-style arguments provide logically sound reasons for normative-individualist policymakers to concern themselves with "aggregate" or "statistical" representation of certain groups in various social, economic, and political arenas, ultimately for the sake of fairness to individuals.

Are there features in such arguments that might lead us, nevertheless, to condemn them as obnoxiously illiberal? What of the fact that they are a form of somewhat fancy social engineering? Many pages of liberal policy gospel—all that concern themselves with maintaining structural and systemic conditions conducive to liberal aims, such as a "free market" (of goods and services, or of ideas) or the separation of church from state—are social engineering; or, rather, they are from the standpoint of all who forbear to claim them as God-given but support them anyway. Are Myrdal-style arguments, then, illiberal because they refuse to hold group members individually responsible for their "choices" to adjust their actions to the appearance of stacked decks and loaded dice, rather than venturing boldly to challenge the odds? Most certainly not, I should think, to anyone who sees that those appearances and their hold on people's minds are the uninterrupted product of a history of wrongful subjugation—who declines to "supplant history with individualized hypotheses about free choice, in which each self chooses her destiny even if it is destitution."[179]

Are the arguments nevertheless illiberal just because they give the need for active government "intervention" (as if the "market" were in all other respects a phenomenon of pre-political nature)

---

[178] See Gunnar Myrdal et al., *An American Dilemma: The Negro Problem and Modern Democracy*, vol. 1 (New York: Harper & Bros., 1944), 75–76; Charles Lawrence, "Segregation 'Misunderstood': The *Milliken* Decision Revisited," *University of San Francisco Law Review* 12 (1977): 15–56, at 36 (1977).

[179] Patricia Williams, "*Metro Broadcasting, Inc. v. FCC*: Regrouping in Singular Times," *Harvard Law Review* 104 (1991): 525, 533.

greater weight than their critics would, relative to presumptive liberal rights to color-blind treatment? Not if we agree that the current social realities are such that reasonable and sincere contestants can differ on the optimal strategies for pursuit of liberal aims.[180] In that case, attributions of illiberality by one side in the debate to the other are self-congratulatory polemic, nothing more.

"Diversity" as justification for affirmative action. Justice Brennan's opinion in *Metro Broadcasting* allowed a governmental aim of "broadcast diversity" to justify certain preferences for minority-owned firms in the competition for broadcast channels. Here is what the Justice wrote by way of explanation:

> The Government's role in distributing the limited number of broadcast licenses is not merely that of a "traffic officer" . . . ; rather it is axiomatic that . . . "the widest possible dissemination of information from diverse and antagonistic sources is essential to the welfare of the public." . . . Safeguarding the public's right to receive a diversity of views and information over the airwaves is therefore an integral component of the [government's] mission. . . . "[T]he people as a whole retain . . . their collective right to have the medium function consistently with the ends and purposes of the First Amendment". . . .
>
> Against this background, we conclude that the interest in enhancing broadcast diversity is, at the very least, an important governmental objective and is therefore a sufficient basis for the [government's] minority ownership policies. Just as a "diverse student body" contributing to a " 'robust exchange of ideas' " is a "constitutionally permissible goal" on which a race-conscious university admissions program

---

[180] See, e.g., Randall Kennedy, "Persuasion and Distrust: A Comment on the Affirmative Action Debate," *Harvard Law Review* 99 (1986): 1327–46, at 1331 (1986) ("[T]he uncertain extent to which affirmative action diminishes . . . blacks must be balanced against the stigmatization that occurs when blacks are virtually absent from important institutions in the society.").

may be predicated (*University of California Regents v. Bakke*, . . . [opinion of J. Powell]), the diversity of views and information on the airwaves serves important First Amendment values. . . . The benefits of such diversity are not limited to the members of minority groups who gain access to the broadcasting industry by virtue of the ownership policies; rather, the benefits redound to all members of the viewing and listening audience. . . .[181]

As stated by Brennan, the aim, which he attributed to Congress, of broadcast diversity is a social-structural aim as true-blue liberal as John Stuart Mill. Critics are surely entitled to argue that governmental favoritism for minority ownership of broadcast channels is not really an effective way to pursue the Millian objective,[182] and furthermore to question the claim that Congress ever considerately found that it was.[183] Such objections, however, cannot suffice to turn Justice Brennan's opinion into a collectivist tract on group rights. Or rather, they can do so only if the claim is that the opinion's liberal trappings are so pitifully weak, so patently phony, that only a secret yen for "equality between groups as such" could credibly explain the result.

No doubt certain assumed facts about group identities played a central part in Justice Brennan's reasoning. The Justice accepted the proposition that moving toward representative numbers of minority-owned broadcasters "would contribute, on average, 'to the 'robust exchange of ideas' "[184]—that "as more minorities gain ownership and policymaking roles in the media, varying perspectives will be more fairly represented on the airwaves."[185] That acceptance committed Brennan, as he recognized, to "the assump-

---

[181] *Metro Broadcasting* at 567–68 (various citations omitted).

[182] See Fried, "*Metro Broadcasting*," 120–21.

[183] Congress's "approval" of the specific FCC policies at issue in *Metro Broadcasting* was given in a rider on an appropriations bill. See *Metro Broadcasting* at 560, 578; Fried, "*Metro Broadcasting*," 117–19.

[184] *Metro Broadcasting* at 579 (quoting *Bakke*, 438 U.S. at 313) (opinion of Powell, J.).

[185] Ibid., 580.

tion that minorities have particular viewpoints and interests worthy of protection."[186] It is doubtless this feature of the *Metro Broadcasting* opinion—this indulgence, as critics might call it, in a belief in group-think or color-think—that most grates on some liberal sensibilities. Yet nothing more is at work here than the intuition that an individual's perspectives and values, understandings and priorities, stand to be inflected in significant ways by that person's social identifiability, self-awareness, acculturation and experience of life in America as, say, an African-American.[187]

It is hard to believe that there are many participants on either side of the affirmative-action debate who do not share such intuitions and sometimes rely on them in thinking and arguing about what is to be done. Justice O'Connor, to choose a handy example, indulged such intuitions at least twice in her *Croson* opinion. She did so when she found not probative of discrimination the "extremely low" presence of minority firms among Richmond area contractors' associations, because, for aught anyone knew, "blacks may be disproportionately attracted to industries other than construction."[188] She did so again when she suggested that the Richmond city council's majority-black composition made the council's set-aside order especially suspect as racial politics.[189] If people's social identifiability as, say, "white" or "black" were not presumed to correlate aggregatively with their experience-based understandings and motivations, neither of these reasonings could even begin to make the slightest sense.

Is there something intrinsically illiberal or malignant in such intuitions? It can be argued that in the United States today, for

---

[186] Ibid., 583.

[187] See, e.g., Williams, "Metro Broadcasting" 529, 533 ("Although [minority] cultures . . . are exceedingly diverse, the most generalizable experience is that of battling cultural suppression if not obliteration, as well as discrimination and exclusion from the larger society."); T. Alexander Aleinikoff, "A Case For Race-Consciousness," *Columbia Law Review* 91:1060–1125, at 1066–72, 1084–86, 1093–95 (1991).

[188] See *Croson*, 488 U.S. at 503; Aleinikoff, "Race-Consciousness," 1100–1102.

[189] See *Croson*, 488 U.S. at 495–96; Aleinikoff, "Race-Consciousness," 1102, 1105.

better or for worse, constitutional law speaks as the country's political creed or dogma, or even as a dominant social language that
helps to establish and entrench the reality it purports to observe
and describe. And so it can be further—it is constantly—argued
that by adopting and propagating the idea that racial identity
makes any kind of significant difference in people's lives, constitutional law would defeat assimilationist goals.[190] That, however,
is an argument of prudence masquerading as one of principle. It
is a contention about what will and will not work to relieve American society of its legacy of racial disharmony and subordination.
And it is, as such, a contested claim. Insofar as the controversy
over preferences is a dispute about means among people sharing
similar goals, a disagreement about the best remedy for a commonly perceived injustice,[191] no one's liberal credentials would
seem to be at stake in it.

I don't mean there are not also mixed up in the affirmative
action debate some sharp conflicts of social vision and value.
Among those who care for individuals and individuality, the goal
of assimilation is itself sharply contested. In the views of many,[192]
socially sanctioned multiculturalism brings evils or dangers of
balkanization that swamp its possible benefits. In the views of others, not only is multiculturalism not the source of such evils, but
it offers the best or only path to individuality on terms of equality
and acceptance that a culturally plural society can offer.[193]

Such contentions point to even deeper group-regarding—yet
liberal—impulses in Justice Brennan's *Metro Broadcasting* testa-
ment than any we have yet noticed. Patricia Williams has cited
Metro Broadcasting for its "recognition of multiculturalism" as a

[190] See, e.g., *Croson*, 488 U.S. at 520–28 (Scalia, J., dissenting).

[191] See, e.g., *Bakke*, 438 U.S. at 407 (Blackmun, J.) ("In order to get beyond
racism, we must first take account of race.").

[192] See, e.g., Cynthia V. Ward, "The Limits of "Liberal Republicanism": Why
Group-Based Remedies and Republican Citizenship Don't Mix," *Columbia Law
Review* 91 (1991): 581–607.

[193] See, e.g., Lani Guinier, "No Two Seats: The Elusive Quest for Political
Equality," *Virginia Law Review* 77 (1991): 1413; Aleinikoff, "Race-Consciousness"; Williams, "Metro Broadcasting."

valued engine of social criticism and, as such, a national (and liberal) social-structural good.[194] In Williams's view, Americans stand in danger of mistaking what is actually a "corporate group identity, radically constraining any sense of individuality" for what they prefer to see as an "ethic of individualism." Williams believes that the dominant ideology has become so "normalized" that we have trouble seeing it as such. She says we need inoculation against confusion of an ideological facade of individualism with the genuine article, and that a good serum would be a cultivated practice of recognition for the off-mainstream cultures and identities that exist in our midst and of respect for "the dynamic power of these groups and . . . their contributions to our civic lives."[195] It was not outlandish for Williams to attribute such views to Justice Brennan. They are, after all, the stuff of which romantic liberal constitutionalism is made.

SUMMATION: WHO IS BRENNAN TO US?

A political outlook or "philosophy" can be described as a parsing of relations among individuals, society at large, and groups within society, with a view to prescribing the relations of all these to the state. Justice Brennan's parsing followed paths well trodden in liberal country. In sum: Individuals are what matter in the end. Individuals are also, however, as a matter of fact, socially constituted, enmeshed in various relations and communities, thought-ways and cultures, institutions and practices. Out of these multiple, overlapping formative contexts, individuality forms itself. Individuals, then, depend for their identities and self-understandings on affiliation and commitment, as they depend for justice, security, and certain other conditions of thriving on public institutions of law and government.

[194] Williams, "Metro Broadcasting," at 545.
[195] Ibid., 534–35; cf. Aleinikoff, "Race Consciousness," 1081–88.

Society, perhaps, devolves toward stratification. Without the state's active, continuing attention to distributions of wealth, status, and power, many individuals suffer constriction of access to the engagements and contestations of social life, and the ones who do are not randomly distributed among social groups with which identities connect. Missing from the scene, then, are their sensibilities, perspectives, articulations of need and value—what Richard Rorty calls their vocabularies and self-descriptions.[196] That absence is itself an insult to justice and a deprivation to everyone. But if absence from the scene of repressed or off-center articulations is one kind of setback to liberal individuality (call it monotony), another is an ascendent articulation's fullness of presence (call it hegemony or totality). For both of these reasons, the good state devotes some of its unique powers to establishing, maintaining, and reproducing social-structural conditions of fair and open cultural and visionary contention, at the same time refusing use of those unique powers for the consolidation of any cultural or ideological party's local or momentary advantage.

Gotten up in the form of principles and doctrines in a specific body of constitutional law, this particular blend of constitutional liberalism surely contains stresses and fissures. It rests on a distinction that it cannot ever quite maintain, between proper governmental support of a particular conception of liberal social structure and illicit governmental imposition of one or another partisan ideology. It is paradoxically committed to commandeer the unique powers of the state for its own partisan cause. But similar difficulties beset all variants of liberalism—finding the right meaning for "neutrality" has long been a main occupation for liberal political philosophers—because committed liberals cannot help but strive to enact their liberalism as constitutional law. Any committed notion of the morally right way for a country to be governed makes us take sides, on the level of constitutional law, about what is good for everyone.[197]

[196] See Richard Rorty, *Contingency, irony, and solidarity* (Cambridge: Cambridge University Press, 1989), 79–80, 94.
[197] See above, pp. 33–34.

That does not mean that the liberal notion of constitutionalism logically necessitates the American practice of partial government by judiciary. The notion surely does require compliance by government actors with constitutional constraints. It does not, all by itself, require enforcement of compliance from the outside. Logically, it is satisfied if governmental actors direct themselves to comply, by honestly considering and specifically resolving any constitutional issues fairly raised by pending political agendas[198]— and, if we believe with Justice Brennan that the Constitution imposes positive duties on the state, honestly assessing from time to time whether all is on the political agenda that compliance requires.

But that is a strong condition, and Americans, evidently, have doubted that their elected lawmakers can be relied on to fulfill it, without policing from a separate high court, staffed by judges imbued with a special set of professionally cultivated expectations of fidelity to law.[199] The fact remains that judicial review is an edifice of liberal political prudence, not a logical entailment of the liberal constitutionalist idea. Moreover, the prudence behind the device has been perennially controversial among American constitutionalists. Participants and commentators from James Bradley Thayer[200] to Robin West[201] have cogently urged that judicial review, by absolving legislatures and electorates from themselves attending to pervasive issues of political morality that we place on the constitutional level, leads in the end to less rather than more effective fidelity to constitutional values.

It is when we place Justice Brennan's particular brand of democratic-liberal constitutionalism on this field of controversy that its most intriguing puzzles appear. The romantic liberal, we said,

[198] See, e.g., William Van Alstyne, "A Critical Guide to *Marbury v. Madison*, *Duke Law Journal* 1969 (1969): 1–45, at 16–29.

[199] See, e.g., Owen Fiss, "Conventionalism," *Southern California Law Review* 58 (1985): 177–97.

[200] See James Bradley Thayer, *John Marshall* (Boston: Houghton-Mifflin, 1901), 106–7.

[201] See West, "Progressive and Conservative Constitutionalism," 717–21.

envisions individuals enabled "to choose and shape their own identities and lives, in part through vistas of possibility opened by contention over aims for the institutions that the people of a country cannot help but share." Democracy, we said, correspondingly becomes "a substantive ideal—a commitment to empower the disempowered and reconnect the alienated." Civil liberties, we said, correspondingly become "both . . . individual right[s] of self-presentation—of efficacious participation or citizenship— and . . . social-structural provisions for imbuing social life with the enrichment . . . of frictional contact with human outlooks and sensibilities other than those to which one has grown accustomed." How is all that to be squared with any degree of government by judiciary?

A judge is not your neighbor in Concord. When he jostles your consciousness, he does not do it by manner, example, or force of personality. He may sometimes succeed in doing it by force of argument, but he *always* does it—he cannot help doing it—by paramount force of arms.[202] (Alexander Hamilton dissembled when he said in *The Federalist No. 78* that judges lack the sword.) That is why one can cogently object that judges doing constitutional review usurp for themselves the political-participatory component of the good life. To which it is plausibly answerable that, in a fallen world, judicial policing of the ground rules helps provide for people generally a surer (if compromised) chance of "participation in change" than the next best alternative.[203] One might even say, with Robin West, that rights "ensure us space to create chaos, disorder, randomness, change, from which we might fashion a new social order."[204] Brennan's view appears to have been something like that.

Late in his career, Justice Brennan opened himself to unconventional and problematic ideas: the high court as a political insti-

---

[202] See Robert M. Cover, "Violence and the Word," *Yale Law Journal* 95 (1986): 1601–29.

[203] On "participation in change," see C. Edwin Baker, *Human Liberty and Freedom of Speech* (Oxford: Oxford University Press, 1989), 47–48.

[204] West, "Narrative, Responsibility and Death," 172.

tution whose members stand always ready, without closure, to revisit questions of constitutional meaning; an appellate court-room as a site of direct encounter between judges and litigants, where judges reach sympathetically for the parties' experiences of the case.[205] Those ideas remain inchoate. If they were ever to take root and find a clear and definite expression in American legal culture and institutions (from here, a development literally beyond imagining), they would rank among Brennan's most memorable contributions to constitutionalism. That the Justice floated them does not, however, change the fact that while he himself held judicial office, the prevailing expectation for that office was far more hierarchical than the vague alternative that he, late in his career, felt moved to seek. Whatever may have been his second thoughts about it, it is fair to say that in practice he took the office as he found it. The Brennan of national memory is destined to be the Brennan who declared the Court "supreme in the exposition of the law of the Constitution."[206]

When Brennan had the votes, his word was law. He laid the law down, when he could, according to the particular political vision he held and believed the Constitution to contain. Those who find in that vision much that is good and right have reason to be thankful that he did so. It is not that we are greatly in Justice Brennan's debt for invention or exposition of a political theory; the political ideas we extract from the Justice's writings can be read elsewhere, more searchingly and systematically presented. Nor can we thank him for an irreversible legacy of rules of constitutional law, because "his" rules are not cast in stone. Yet, however much the rules laid down by the Warren Court, or any court, may be redone or replaced, the river does not flow upstream and historic transformations in the terms of American constitutional debate can never be annulled.[207] It is not only by its rulings, after

[205] Brennan, "Reason and Passion," 15, 19–21.

[206] Cooper v. Aaron, 358 U.S. 1 (1958). For Brennan's authorship, see chapter 1, n. 8.

[207] See Owen Fiss, "A Life Lived Twice," *Yale Law Journal* 100 (1991): 1117–29, at 1127 (observing that Justice Brennan's opinions "define the field on which the present Court operates").

all, that the Court affects life in America and the course of American history. The Justices have in fact held a goodly portion of the power to set the terms of political debate in this country, and it may matter incalculably which ideas get respect there and which do not.

Justice Brennan's successor on the bench, Justice David Souter, said this in his eulogy:

> One thousand three hundred and sixty of the opinions set out in those books are his. . . . If our next decision is meant to follow the course he set, we will reach out to him, and if we will not accept his direction we will have to grapple with him. But year after year, in subject after subject of the national law, we will either accept the inheritance of his thinking, or we will have to face him squarely and make good on our challenge to him. And so there are no good-byes to be said now to William Brennan the Justice; we shall deal with him many times again.[208]

Among judicial statements of political principles and ideas may be some that will one day figure as prophetic. Nothing limits the category to maverick views first uttered as dissents. It may extend as well to syntheses that gain and hold the field for a time before they suffer eclipse by overruling and other forms of discreditation. They, too, remain available for recovery. Even so, to praise Justice Brennan as a visionary, a prophet, would be to trivialize his contribution to American constitutional history. His status is altogether different. He was a framer.

[208] David H. Souter, "In Memoriam—William J. Brennan, Jr.," *Harvard Law Review* 111 (1997): 1–2.

AUGUST 29, 1961. A Tuesday. My first or second week on the job as law clerk to Justice Brennan. I caught a first glimpse of my new boss at work, conducting (of all things) an oral argument in chambers.

The case was *Board of Education of New Rochelle* v. *Taylor*.[1] The name may not ring a bell, but *Taylor* was a historic case, the first to impose a constitutional responsibility on a northern school district to desegregate its schools. True, the Supreme Court did not exactly decide the case itself. It was a federal trial court that did the heavy lifting, when it found on the evidence that the Board of Education in New Rochelle, N.Y., had made various decisions about school zoning, transfers, and building replacement for the purpose, and with the effect, of maintaining its Lincoln Elementary School as a "racially segregated" school—one that would take in as nearly as possible an exclusively black population, and by doing so would help to keep a lid on black enrollment at surrounding, predominantly white schools.[2] Concluding that the city had thereby denied equal protection of the laws to black children assigned by residence to Lincoln, the trial judge had ordered the city to allow those children to transfer to other city schools with available space (providing their own transportation), and to assist the transfer process by annual mailings of transfer application forms.[3] A sharply divided panel of appeals court judges, reviewing the trial record, found that it supported the trial judge's actions.[4]

---

[1] 82 S. Ct. 10 (1961) (Brennan, Circuit Justice); see id. at 11 (denying application for a stay of the trial court's mandate); Taylor v. Bd. of Educ., 195 F. Supp. 231, 240–41 (S.D.N.Y.1961) (prescribing remedy), *aff'd*, 294 F.2d 36 (1961); Taylor v. Bd. of Educ., 191 F. Supp. 181, 197 (S.D.N.Y. 1961) (finding constitutional violation).

[2] See *Taylor*, 191 F. Supp. at 183–92; see also *Taylor*, 195 F. Supp. at 235 (1961).

[3] See 191 F. Supp. at 183.

[4] See *Taylor*, 294 F.2d at 38–39.

These were trail-blazing decisions. Never before had courts found unconstitutional segregation in a district where all schools were attended by students of both races and there was not in effect any law or ordinance reserving some schools for whites only and others for blacks. The equal protection clause was coming North.[5]

Historic as it was in the annals of school desegregation, the *Taylor* case was not to become a hot item on the Supreme Court's calendar for the year 1961–62. (The Court's headliners that year were *Baker v. Carr*,[6] the decision that put federal judges into the business of applying constitutional equality standards to state legislative districting and apportion schemes, and *Engel v. Vitale*,[7] the first case in which teacher-led school prayers were held to be an unconstitutional establishment of religion.) New Rochelle's petition to the Supreme Court to take up its case for further review arrived during the Court's summer recess. In August, that petition lay waiting, along with hundreds of others, for a response from the Justices sometime around the first Monday in October. Meanwhile, New Rochelle was looking for someone to excuse it from compliance with the trial judge's remedial order until the Supreme Court should decide whether to review the case; the city was seeking what is called a temporary "stay" of that order. Having been turned down in this quest by both the trial judge and the appeals panel, on the rather obvious ground that compliance with the on-request transfer requirement for the coming year would be easy for the city, whereas a year's postponement could be prejudicial to lifetime educational interests of the plaintiffs,[8] New Rochelle was now directing a last-ditch application for a stay to the Supreme Court.

[5] See John Kaplan, "Segregation Litigation in the Schools—Part I: The New Rochelle Experience," *Northwestern University Law Review* 58 (1963–64): 1–72, at 4: John Kaplan, "Segregation Litigation in the Schools—Part II: The General Northern Problem," *Northwestern University Law Review* 58 (1963–64): 157.

[6] 369 U.S. 186 (1962).

[7] 370 U.S. 421 (1962).

[8] See ibid. at 40; *Taylor*, 195 F. Supp. at 238–39.

Because the Court was on its summer break, the city's application was, by the usual practice, routed for action to a single Justice—Justice Brennan, as it happened. Reasons for rejecting the
stay application seemed obvious and overwhelming. The Supreme Court has repeatedly declared its extreme reluctance to
make a prevailing party wait for relief while it decides whether to
take up a case for review (a process that can take many months),
especially when both a trial court and an appeals panel have already agreed on both the defendant's liability in the case and the
inappropriateness of delaying relief.[9] Justice Brennan nevertheless saw fit to set the matter for oral argument.

I have never heard, before or since, of an oral argument on a
single-justice application for a stay order, and I never did find out
exactly why Justice Brennan called for one on this occasion. He
must have wanted to be careful with the matter, and one can see
why he might have.

From today's vantage point, the New Rochelle case looks like
a simple one for the Supreme Court, even if it may not have been
so simple for the trial court. It was the trial judge who had to
decide whether the evidence in the case sufficiently proved that
a government agency had intentionally acted for the specific purpose of concentrating black pupils in "their own" public schools.
The evidence was circumstantial. No New Rochelle official testi-
fied to having acted for the purpose of shepherding as many
blacks and as few whites as possible into Lincoln, or for the purpose of preserving large white majorities at other schools. The
judge had to infer the segregatory motive from the history of the
various actions taken and choices made over the years by New
Rochelle authorities, as shown by the documentary and testimo-
nial evidence put together by the plaintiffs and their lawyers. But
once he did reach that conclusion, and once the appeals panel
blessed it, the case starts to look like a no-brainer for the Supreme
Court. Government action intentionally designed to keep blacks

---

[9] See Magnum Import Co. v. Coty, 262 U.S. 159, 163 (1923); Graver v.
Tank & Mfg Co. v. Linde Air Prods. Co., 336 U.S. 271, 275 (1949).

segregated from whites, we now know, directly violates the anti-discrimination principle established by the historic *Brown* decision of 1954. Obviously, the Supreme Court denies review.

That was not, however, obvious at the time of which we speak. In August of 1961, no one was sure of how the Court might respond to the New Rochelle case. The *Brown* case itself, like all the other segregation cases that had by that time come before the Court, involved a so-called "dual" school system in which every school in the system was strictly reserved by law either to whites or to nonwhites. That was a kind of arrangement that existed only in the south and in a few other scattered areas of the country. Elsewhere, when a locality contained more than one school at a particular grade level, students were normally assigned on the basis of residence, using a map of attendance zones for the various schools. It was widely known to be common for managers of such nominally "unitary" systems to use devices such as attendance zone remappings and discretionary transfers to cater to their white constituencies' perceived strong desires to have their own children in white-dominated schools. If the Supreme Court were to read the *Brown* decision as prohibiting that sort of *sub rosa* indulgence of racism, then the impact of the *Brown* decision would be felt countrywide. There was real uncertainty in 1961 about whether the Court was prepared to move in such a direction. Justice Brennan may not have taken for granted that a majority of his judicial brethren would vote to deny review in *Taylor*. Perhaps, in anticipation of the full Court's consideration of the matter, he wished to make certain that the record showed his own meticulous regard for New Rochelle's concerns.

For whatever reason, he scheduled the oral argument. When the moment arrived, I was surprised to see the Boss himself trudging out to the hallway to usher the lawyers into his inner office, where fellow clerk Roy Schotland and I composed a small gallery at the back of the room. Pulling off his own coat and hanging it over the back of his chair, Justice Brennan motioned the visitors to do likewise. To the man from New Rochelle: "Oh *is* it [your first visit to the Court]? Did you bring any family along? How about a tour later on? We'll set it up." To both lawyers: "Sit down, sit down, make yourselves comfortable. We're going to be informal here. Can I get you some tea?" After a bit, kindly, to the man from New Rochelle: "Let's go ahead if you're ready." Nervous and formal, the city's lawyer launched into his prepared argument. Brennan listened attentively, intervening several times with cordial and sympathetic questions. It was over in ten minutes. Brennan turned to the respondents' lawyer. "Mr. Marshall?"

Perhaps because his case against the stay was so simple and obvious as to leave him little to say, Mr. Marshall got off to what seemed to me a halting start.[10] The Justice was quickly on him with a direct challenge. "Suppose you did have to wait a year for relief. What would be so terrible about that?" A noticeable pause; Mr. Marshall looking a little downcast, hunching forward in his seat, palms on knees. Then the response, Marshall still looking at his shoe tops: "Justice Brennan, my clients have been waiting a long time." (Maybe he said, "my people." Maybe he said, "long enough.") "These other folks, won't hurt 'em if they have to hustle a little." Bingo. End of argument. End of Introduction to Appellate Advocacy. I thought: They never taught me that at Harvard.

Soon Justice Brennan was escorting the lawyers out of the office. Returning to his desk, he sat musing. Then, looking up at us, two young men he had barely met and did not know but simply and unguardedly took on as pals worthy of his confidence, the Irish grin lighting his face, mock-conspiratorially: "Well, guys, what do you suppose we're going to do about *that*?" One or the other of us offered to draft a memorandum denying the stay application, but the Justice said it wouldn't be necessary and proceeded to do it himself, effortlessly I'm sure. A few months later,

[10] Thanks to Roy Schotland for help in reconstructing exactly what happened next.

the full Court denied the city's petition for review, bringing the case to an end.[11]

To me, today, the memory of that August afternoon speaks of Justice Brennan's kindliness, his humor, his verve, his graciousness, his immense and touching open-heartedness. It speaks of his resolve: the way he conveyed to us (with hardly a word) the firmness of his sense that the principle of *Brown* must hold in New Rochelle no less than in Little Rock. It speaks of his friendship: a blessing and a joy to all upon whom it fell—and we are legion—into which I was that day inducted. It speaks of his trust and his optimism: the way it went without saying, as any of his clerks can tell you, that we pals would want to be with him on the side of the angels—the side of the slighted, the denigrated, the unheard, the ungreat, the forgotten, and the condemned. It speaks of Brennan's special greatness as a judge—judicial greatness, in his case, having so much consisted in the fight he fought so ably to make the law look out for the dignity and "intrinsic worth" of every person.[12]

Years later, after his retirement, Justice Brennan and I together recalled the events of that day. I asked him whether he could say with any certainty whether that was the first time he and Thurgood Marshall had met close up—had begun, so to speak, to take each other's measure, person to person.[13] The Justice mulled my question over for a while, then answered that he was pretty sure it was the first time, except possibly for a brief introduction at some large social gathering. I felt the undeserved glow that descends on those who've been idly present at the creation of some-

---

[11] See Board of Educ. v. Taylor, 368 U.S. 940 (1961).

[12] Gregg v. Georgia, 428 U.S. 153, 229 (1976) (Brennan, J., dissenting).

[13] Thurgood Marshall, of course, was the lead lawyer for the NAACP Legal Defense & Educational Fund in 1961. A number of distinguished LDF attorneys, including Constance Baker Motley and Jack Greenberg, had represented the *Taylor* plaintiffs at various stages of the proceedings. I should point out that Marshall had argued at least one important case before the full Supreme Court since Brennan's arrival there in 1956. I have in mind *Cooper v. Aaron*, 358 U.S. 1 (1958), for which see chapter 1, n. 8.

thing they take to be historically and morally important. That was after the time when Justice Marshall saluted the freshly retired Justice Brennan as "my brother."[14] It was before the time in Arlington National Cemetery when, from my obstructed-view position, Marshall's was the only tombstone I could see in close neighborhood to where Brennan's apparently would be.

[14] Wendy Benjaminson, *Justice Remembered as Voice of Compassion*, Associated Press, July 20, 1990.